THE LIVING WORD
VOLUME 2

How The Gospels Work

WILLIAM J. O'MALLEY, S.J.

PAULIST PRESS
New York, N.Y./Ramsey, N.J.

I would be sorely remiss if I did not acknowledge my debt of gratitude to Gerald Blaszczak, S.J., who toiled painstakingly through these pages with the keen eye and mind of a scholar, with a kind patience not usual in an academician for a popularizer. I must leave it to the Subject of these books to repay him.

Acknowledgments

The poem "The Creation" is taken from *God's Trombones* by James Weldon Johnson, copyright 1927 by The Viking Press, Inc., copyright renewed 1955 by Grace Nail Johnson, and reprinted by permission of The Viking Press. Excerpts from *The New Testament: An Introduction* by Norman Perrin are reprinted by permission of Harcourt Brace Jovanovich, Inc. Passages from *Gospel Parallels* by Burton H. Throckmorton are copyrighted © 1949, 1957, 1967 by The Division of Christian Education of the National Council of Churches of Christ in the U.S.A. and are reprinted by permission of Thomas Nelson, Inc., Publishers.

Library of Congress
Catalog Card Number 80-80534

ISBN: 0-8091-9559-3

Published by Paulist Press
Editorial Office: 1865 Broadway, New York, N.Y. 10023
Business Office: 545 Island Road, Ramsey, N.J. 07446

Printed and bound in the
United States of America

For
MY MOTHER
that high priestess
of metaphor and myth

CONTENTS

PART ONE

How the Gospel Became the Gospels

1

GOSPEL:
HISTORY AND FAITH

Jesus didn't write the gospels. The first Christian communities did. Strangely, many good Christians are rather surprised when they realize that the Church came *before* the gospels. Of course they realize that Jesus didn't write things like "And then Jesus said," but they are shocked, even scandalized, when some seemingly fanatic apostate suggests that even every word quoted by the evangelists as coming from Jesus' mouth is not necessarily a perfectly accurate quotation. Somehow they would like to believe that someone in the backhills of first-century Palestine had a secret tape recorder and took everything down. If this were so, how would they explain the following quotations as "recorded" by three evangelists:

MATTHEW 24: 19–20	MARK 13:11	LUKE 21: 14–15
When they deliver you up do not be anxious how you are to speak or what you are to say; for what you are to say will be given to you in that hour; for it is not you who speak, but the Spirit of your Father speaking through you.	And when they bring you to trial and deliver you up, do not be anxious beforehand what you are to say; but say whatever is given you in that hour for it is not you who speak but the Holy Spirit.	Settle it therefore in your minds, not to meditate beforehand how to answer; for I will give you a mouth and wisdom, which none of your adversaries will be able to withstand or contradict.

LUKE 12: 11–12

And when they bring
you before the syna-
gogues and the rulers
and the authorities, do
not be anxious how or
what you are to answer
or what you are to say
for the Holy Spirit will
teach you in that very
hour what you ought to
say.

Although each of the quotations says substantially the same thing, which one is the statement of the *real* Jesus? The absolutely accurate words? When people of simple faith encounter such a question—and this one is relatively uncomplicated compared to some of the differences in reportage we will see later—they are not merely confused, but their faith is terribly shaken, not just in the Church or the gospels, but in Jesus himself. They might say, "If we don't have the absolutely accurate words of Jesus, then maybe the whole thing is a hoax! Maybe the whole thing is just 'made-up'!"

I am completely convinced that the whole thing was not just "made-up" or a hoax, but I am also convinced that the gospels are not absolutely accurate reportage of historical events, written at the very moment they occurred, like a modern TV news program. They were never intended to be. They were the recording of a myth—a way of telling the truth when the truth is too big for words.

No one can self-consciously invent a myth out of his or her head—not in the sense we have been using that word. It must be rooted in the real. It must arise out of the consciousness of a people and correspond to the-way-things-are as those people see things. In this sense, myth is meant to express their fundamental understandings of themselves and life. If the myth does that, it is true and valid and effective; if it doesn't, it just dies. The myth of atoms for instance, describes a reality which can't be seen but whose effects can be seen. When we act as if the atom really looked like the Niels Bohr model, it works. Similarly, when we act as if the myth of progress were literally true—that anyone can be President if one works hard enough, that things are all getting better—a lot of things actually do get better.

In the same way, the central figure of the New Testament myth was a

historical figure: a man who, we know from testimony, preached, healed, made certain claims about himself, was executed by a Roman official whose name we know, and returned to life in a way that convinced his followers. We have testimony to his historical existence from non-Christian writers, *e.g.*, Josephus, Pliny, Tacitus, Suetonius. In fact, we know he existed just as we know Socrates existed, and on the same kind of evidence. But we also know that over the course of 2,000 years this man's life and ideas have enriched the lives of countless millions of human beings. The myth validates itself in living it out.

There is a crucial distinction Laurence Perrin makes between "historical" and "historic." By "historical" one means the actual event, what happened; by "historic" one means the event-as-interpreted, what it means in the whole perspective of human life and human significance. For instance, during the Civil War a great many men fought and died at Gettysburg, Pennsylvania. There was actual gunfire; certain men stood on certain spots; particular individuals died here and there. It was historical; it actually happened. But the event was just one more battle, just one more occurrence, until Abraham Lincoln interpreted it, put it into the whole perspective of what the war was all about and what human liberty is all about. As Mabel Lang has said, "In a very real sense, the chief reason that we remember what men *did* at Gettsburg is what Lincoln *said* there." The historical event became historic when Lincoln showed its meaning.

The death of Jesus was historical; it actually happened. But without the gospels, without interpretation, without someone to bring out its significance, it would be just one more man who died unjustly on a Roman cross. Facts and historical data are not enough. We listen to historical data on the TV news every night—so-and-so shot someone, such-and-such company is raising prices, this or that product may cause cancer. But what does it all mean? Where does it all fit? So a commentator comes on and does the best he or she can to tell us. St. Paul and the evangelists tried to do exactly the same thing.

The gospels are not a biography; they are a message, an interpretation of events. Granted the historical, biographical details about what Jesus did, what do they mean to us? The gospel was a historic message which Paul could proclaim in a single sentence:

> *First and foremost, I handed on to you the facts which had been imparted to me: that Christ died for our sins, in accordance with the*

scriptures; that he was buried; that he was raised to life on the third day, according to the scriptures; and that he appeared to Cephas, and afterwards to the Twelve . . . and in the end, he appeared even to me.

I Cor. 15: 3–9

Facts are not enough for understanding; they have to be interpreted, put into the full context of our present lives. In a sense, every priest does this every Sunday when an event from Scripture is read, and he rises, with his own talents and limitations, to try to explain what the event means to his audience. In interpreting an event, one must explain who this person is, what he or she said and did, but one must also show the importance of this event beyond its mere occurrence: how this event should indeed change minds, change lives, change the whole course of history. Therefore Paul and the evangelists spoke of the "historical" Jesus as he actually was but also of the "historic" Jesus as he was interpreted, his significance for future generations. And the authenticity of their interpretation is guaranteed by the inspiration of the Spirit of Jesus, still living in their midst.

Therefore, the New Testament myth—again, in the sense we have been using that word—is built around actual concrete, historical persons. But the myth, the message of the gospels, is proved not by whether Jesus actually did this or that miracle as it is described or by whether he actually said these particular words in this particular order. It is validated by whether the message works when incorporated into life, whether the all-out Christian's life is enriched by the message. The core assertion of the gospel is that Jesus is the quintessence of God and man, sent to announce and inaugurate the kingdom, the unconditional love of our Father for those who have no hope of salvation by Jewish standards. He is the revelation of God, his Word. He is the "best of us," and by living his life one finds joy.

As Will Rogers said so well, if theologians would spend more time explaining to us the meaning of our Savior's message and less time trying to figure out his means of arrival and departure, we'd all be a lot better off!

One particular event recorded in the gospel narrative which most scholars agree is legendary is the episode of the Magi. The event is described rather tersely: The men are not kings but they do have rich presents; they are not described as being one white, one black, one oriental—though that would do no harm, since it fits perfectly into the reason the event was inserted into the gospel anyway. What the evangelist was concerned with was not historical kings but with another facet of the message: Just as Jesus came to redeem the poor, uneducated, Jewish shepherds, he also came to

redeem the rich, learned, Gentiles. All peoples were a concern for Christ, and therefore they should be a concern for all Christians. And if all of us lived out that facet of the myth, we would be far better off than we are. Those who try it find it works.

Even as sophisticated a writer as the author of Luke-Acts could write about both the historical and the mythic in exactly the same way. The evangelist can distort historical events, as was probably the case with the apocalyptic occurrences at the Crucifixion; he can even invent them, as was probably the case with the Magi. The test of their validity is whether they truly extend the truth of the myth. As Perrin says, "The birth of Jesus did change forever the possibilities for a man living in the world; his ascension is a way of saying that there is now a futurity for human existence in the world that was not there before. The myth is a vividly pictorial way of interpreting the history."

The New Testament writers use narrative to interpret events. For instance, Matthew lifts details right out of Psalms 69 and 22, which were concerned with the righteous sufferer and God's vindication of him, and inserts them into his version of the events at Calvary.

MATTHEW 27	PSALMS
"They offered him wine to drink, mingled with gall; but when he tasted it, he would not drink it." (v. 34)	"They gave me poison to eat instead; when I was thirsty they gave me vinegar to drink." (69:21)
"And when they crucified him, they divided his garments among them by casting lots. . . ." (v. 35)	They divide my garments among them and cast lots for my clothes." (22:18)
"And those who passed by derided him, wagging their heads and saying, 'You who would destroy the temple and build it in three days, save yourself! If you are the Son of God come down from the cross. . . .'" (v. 39)	"All who see me jeer at me, they toss their heads and sneer." (22:7)
"He trusts in God; let God deliver him now, if he desires him; for he said, 'I am the Son of God.'" (v. 43)	"He relied on Yahweh, let Yahweh save him! If Yahweh is his friend, let Him rescue him!" (22:8)

What does it matter if some loathesome little sadist actually, historically, did or did not blaspheme with his own scriptures over a dying man? These narrative details may or may not be true at the level of factual history, but

they are included because *ipso facto* they put the crucifixion of Jesus into its truest context: Jesus is the righteous sufferer whom God vindicated, and therefore is the fulfillment of Psalms 69 and 22. Moreover, the Jesus-event looks not only backward to the psalms but forward to the present when the evangelist was writing, when dedicated Christians were living out not only the life of Jesus but his sufferings as well.

Therefore, the New Testament is *history*, both *historical* and *historic*, i.e., the historical interpreted by means of myth: narration, hyperbole, irony—the whole treasury of figurative communication. It is a method which narrates the events in such a way that the narration itself (even if details are invented) is a commentary and an interpretation of the historical events. Therefore, if one of the evangelists diverges from the others in his choice of words or in depicting the audience or setting in which the same speech is given or in the placement of a particular event in his overall narrative, the choice is motivated by his conviction that some nuance or facet of the basic message will be better served by his placement—whether or not this event historically occurred here or there.

Some events of the gospels are actually historical, some are mythic, some are merely legendary (like the angels at Bethlehem), but the *whole complex is historic.* Does this mean that we should drop angels from Christmas cards? No more than we should drop those stylized hearts from Valentine cards. Just because one's attempts to capture the uncapturable are inadequate does not mean that they are bad. The gospels are, in a sense, sermons—designed to elicit in the reader the response of faith to the core truth which they propose and thereby to enrich his or her life. As Perrin declares:

> The parables of Jesus were remembered and handed on as tradition within the Christian communities, but as they were handed on they were reinterpreted both by changes within the texts of the parables themselves and also by the addition of new conclusions or explanations to them. Then, when the evangelists incorporated them into their gospels, they introduced further changes to make them express the meaning they saw in them. . . . A fundamental aspect of the New Testament texts is that they are in no small part the end product of a long and constant process of interpretation and reinterpretation.

Just as Peter, in his homily on Pentecost, felt free to reinterpret the prophet Joel, so the author of Luke-Acts might well have done a little

reinterpreting of his own of Peter's reinterpretation. And any priest who composes a homily on that passage in Acts does a little more reinterpreting himself. The criterion of truth is whether the homily really speaks of the way things really are—not merely as one individual sees them, but as God has consistently shown us that *he sees* things. It is, like the work of the prophets, interpreting the historical in the name of God.

Similarly, once the early Church had the gospel of Mark, why did they bother writing three more? There is no essential change in the core statement of Mark when the reader moves to Matthew and Luke and John. But each of the evangelists, as we shall see later in more detail, took the historical facts and the interpretations made before him and saw different shadings, different insights into what Jesus said and did which would help his audience. For instance, Mark was probably written for non-Palestinian Christians who were formerly pagans, probably Romans. He explicitly translates Aramaic words into Greek for them; he has less concern than the others to connect the message of Jesus with the Old Testament; he underscores the meaning of the gospel for newly baptized pagans, especially those who suffer persecution for their faith.

From similar evidence, we can legitimately infer that Matthew was written for Jewish converts. His central purpose seems to be to show conclusively that Jesus is the Messiah Jews hoped for. His division into five books parallels the five books of the Jewish law. He frequently quotes the Old Testament as evidence that Jesus is the new Moses and the Christian community is the new Israel.

Luke, the most literary of the gospels, seems by the elegance of its Greek to be directed at a more learned audience, and it is, indeed, addressed to a prominent man named Theophilus. Luke's reassessment of the gospel message could well have been motivated at least in part by his attempt to understand why the expected Second Coming had not occurred, since he softpedals references to its nearness and emphasizes that its time is quite indefinite. He writes primarily for Gentiles and therefore never uses the Aramaic words common in Matthew, like "rabbi" or "Abba" or "hosanna." Instead he calls Jesus "Teacher" or "Master." As is obvious from his addition of parables which the others do not seem to have known about, he was concerned about interpreting the message of Jesus about the poor, outcasts, women, and Gentiles.

The version by John, from the style of the Greek, seems to have been written in large part by an author or authors more used to thinking—and perhaps even dictating—in Aramaic. In John, we have no parables, no

simple moral instructions, no controversies about the law with Jewish officials. Instead, we have much allegory and involved symbolism, which leads scholars to believe that the author was trying to translate the message into terms which could be understood by those familiar with current Hellenistic religious and philosophical ideas and language. It is, then, the reflection on the message by a theologian with a strong philosophical, symbolic, even mystical interest.

When each successive evangelist began his work, he did not set out to "correct" the original. Apparently, each thought that the gospel versions as he knew them failed to render Jesus fully, in a way easily comprehensible to his own particular audience. For this reason, he used some new material he had discovered in the traditions of his own community and reworked the old. Like four different artists painting the same subject, each gives us a unique insight into one and the same Jesus. It would be quibbling to say that their reinterpretations of their common material was illegitimate.

WHY SO LATE?

When I first began to study theology and Scripture, it was a great strain on my faith when I learned that most reputable Scripture scholars put the date of Mark, the earliest gospel version, somewhere between 60–70 A.D. about thirty years after the events it describes. That gap made me nervous. Why did they wait so long? A lot of distortion can creep into mouth-to-ear chains of communications; Why hadn't they "locked up" the definitive version as soon as possible after it actually, historically happened?

There were several reasons why the gospel message was passed along orally rather than in written form. First of all, the early Christians were not very "literary" people; in fact many of them were probably illiterate. Education in the first century was confined mostly to the wealthy and aristocratic and, at first, there was no value in writing everything down when there were so few converts who could read it. Secondly, and more importantly, such people were far more willing to accept testimony when it was delivered face-to-face. Moreover, the early audience for the gospel had an extraordinary training in memory devices—which is one reason scholars suspect that the core of the beatitudes, which depend on a formula, and the parables, which have a story form, are the closest we have to accurate recollections of Jesus' actual words. Such people were not distracted as we are by the glut of television entertainments, newspapers, magazines, and billboards. They had

a small—and therefore easily learned—body of literature which was their whole library of religion, culture, and entertainment. When you have nothing else to do in your spare time, whether you spend it whittling or retelling stories, you tend to become very good at it.

But the most important reason for the delay in writing it all down was surely the fact that, as we have seen, many of the earliest Christians believed that the end of the world was at hand. It hardly seems profitable to write history when you believe that history is about to end. Paul wrote letters—the earliest parts of the New Testament—not because he hoped that they would be preserved for many generations but because he was doing exactly the work of the gospel—interpreting the message of Jesus to particular audiences and their particular problems at the moment. His interpretations were written simply because he was in one place and his audiences were in other places. He would far rather have handled the interpretations orally, but that was impossible. Paul probably never even dreamed he was writing "Scripture." Later, as the Second Coming seemed to be delayed, his writings became even more valuable as they in their turn were studied and reinterpreted for new situations.

It is most likely that many of the oral communications about the life and the words of Jesus were put together in small written collections which centered around a common theme: poverty and riches, seed parables, various beatitudes—all statements which various witnesses recalled Jesus making, brought together in little scrolls—even though Jesus may have spoken them on many different occasions. These were for the convenience of preachers and catechists. Finally Mark collected such little booklets, combined them and arranged them into a "full" treatment of the life and message of Jesus.

There were three crucial reasons why such overall treatments became necessary. First, the validity of the message depended on the eyewitnesses who had been present when it was given and lived. The first apostles and disciples were the foundation of the Church. But when these witnesses began to die, either in persecutions or from natural causes, their witness had to be concentrated into documents in order to preserve it authentically after there were no more eyewitnesses to validate what was said about Jesus' life and message.

Secondly, the early Christian community was dominated by the belief that the end was at hand. When that event just didn't happen, the community had to sit down and re-examine, to make a re-assessment of their

overliteral interpretation of what apocalyptic statements by Jesus revealed of God's plan. They believed utterly that the new order had come in Jesus, but they were faced with the equally undeniable evidence that the old order had not yet passed away. They began to see that it would be a matter of time before the new kingdom would be fulfilled and that most of them would live full lives and die before the Second Coming occurred. Therefore, the focus of their reinterpretations of the message had to shift from preparing for the immediate end to history and settle on understanding how the message should be applied to an ordinary life.

Thirdly, there was just the natural inclination to reflect on and probe more deeply into the meaning of the person and message of the most important Person in human history. If the message is "Jesus is Lord," then what is he like? In what concrete ways can I, in a different place and time, be more like him? If Jesus fulfills all the expectations of the Hebrew scriptures, how? These are questions the written gospels were meant to begin answering.

Finally, as the Church began to spread in the Greco-Roman world, interpretation of the gospel message became subject to influence by all kinds of foreign religious and philosophic movements. Thus, it was in danger of being adapted and reinterpreted in ways different or even contrary to Jesus' original intention and to the experience of the first apostolic witnesses. It was necessary to assure that its basic message was rooted in the life and ideas of the historically real Jesus. In a sense, the Church does the same thing even today, testing each new adaptation against the recorded intentions of its founder.

The word "gospel" translates the Greek *euangelion*. It means "good news" pronounced by a herald who made the news official, by the very act of announcement. When the herald spoke, the new king officially took power. So when Mark begins his book with the words, "The beginning of the Good News [*evangelion*] about Jesus Christ, the Son of God," those of his readers who were Jewish instantly heard echoes of the prophet Isaiah:

> *How beautiful on the mountains*
> *are the feet of one who brings Good News,*
> *who heralds peace, brings happiness,*
> *proclaims salvation,*
> *and tells Zion,*
> *"Your God is king!"*
>
> Isaiah 52:7

FAITH

The gospels, then, are a collection of things Jesus actually, historically did say and do. But they also contain some events and sayings which the early Christian community made up and "had" Jesus do and say—to demonstrate how Jesus would have acted, *consistent with his basic historical message*, in situations he did not in fact encounter but which troubled the people who came after him. They were also dotted with pious legends which, though historically "untrue," nonetheless were used as vehicles to fill out other facets of the message (as the Magi were). As Catholic Christians, we believe that the Spirit guided the Church to understand and describe the person and mission of Jesus in terms which Jesus himself may never have known or used.

But doesn't this raise a credibility problem? Who knows which is which? Someone may well ask, "Who is this person to tell me what Jesus *would* have said if such-and-such a problem had come up?"

In answer to the first point, there *are* men and women who can give a pretty good idea which elements of the gospels are most likely completely historical, which are extensions of the message to later problems and the reasons why this extension was done, and which are legends and what facet of the message they were intended to fill out. Their answers are found in commentaries on Sacred Scripture, like the enormously detailed but very readable *Jerome Biblical Commentary*. Any serious reader of the Scriptures can find the level of any saying or event of the Bible—from Genesis to Revelation—in one of the commentaries. Although scholars may disagree, although they almost always hedge with words like "more than likely," they are scrupulously honest.

The answer to the "who is he" question is a bit more difficult, since the attitude it betrays at least suggests that, like Thomas, the objector is not going to be convinced unless he himself puts his physical fingers into Jesus' physical wounds. And yet as John says in the only beatitude in his gospel: "Blessed are those who have not seen and yet believe." As I said before, only the person who has really *lived* the gospel can really *read* the gospels. A myth is, after all, validated only when a person lives it out and finds it actually works, actually enriches his or her life.

The Christian believer is not the naive simpleton many non-believers would like to picture. Surely Aquinas and Thomas More and John XXIII are evidence of that. One needs only to read a few pages of Teilhard de Chardin

or Bernard Lonergan to find that brilliant people have believed, and passionately so. But "despite" their brilliance, they are willing to accept the life and death of this Jesus as having cosmic implications in their own lives. They are willing because they have lived the message fully, and they have found in the living a joy that other people did not have.

The message of the myth has been even further verified by their profound experiences of the living God in prayer. Their gospel-enriched lives and their encounter with God proved beyond proof that the evangelists who reinterpreted and fabricated had every right to do so—since their embellishments are absolutely consistent with the basic message of Jesus and their own experience of God. If the words of Jesus were inspired by the Spirit within him, the words of the early Christian community were inspired in their turn by that same Spirit, whom Jesus left to them.

When I was wrestling with this crisis of faith myself in my first year of theological studies, I remember that the only thing that kept me going for a long while was the fact that my two Scripture professors still said Mass every morning. With unaccustomed wisdom I said to myself, "Those two men know more loopholes and problems about the Scriptures than I'll ever know, but they still pray. They still say Mass. There must be an answer to this someplace, and I just haven't found it." And there was: living it and praying it.

The non-believer is usually someone who has not had that experience of God indisputably communicating to him or her. If it had been communicated, such a person would obviously have become a believer! Such a man or woman can read the Bible as the record of an ancient people—filled with myths, poems, fictional narratives, legal papers, advice, etc.—just as he or she would read the collected *monumenta* of the Egyptians or Bantus and Mayans. It is a fascinating academic study. But only the believer can find the *intended* meaning.

The man or woman of faith—the fully convinced believer—is more like one who has "been to the mountain and seen." The believer is not always so sure *what* he or she has seen, but they are sure they have seen something. The believer has had an experience of an encounter with a personal force which blew his or her mind. It was more real than any communication with another, more exhilarating than any daydream, more startling than merely being "struck by an idea." Such prayerful men and women believed that the active presence of God is working in this structure of myths. They believe that the same Person who speaks to them in this strange and

incommunicable way also speaks through the words and events and symbols of the Scriptures. For the non-believer, reading the Scripture is like eavesdropping on a conversation between friends. For the believer, it is like being in on the conversation as one of the friends.

If you haven't had this realization, if you haven't had the mind-blowing experience of seeing it all fall together, you will just have to take the word of those who have.

FINDING THE INTENDED MEANING

The gospels are not unbiased accounts. They were written by men of faith in Jesus for men and women of faith in Jesus. Trying to describe the difference in the impact of reading the Scriptures after one believes—as opposed to reading them before one believed—is like trying to explain the ecstasy of falling in love to a five-year-old. One has almost to get into the disciples' shoes and walk around in them to duplicate, even remotely, the enormity of what they intended to say and what their faith-filled audience heard.

To find the correct interpretation of a Scripture passage means to find the interpretation that God and the author intended. The author, like the prophets, was interpreting events in the light of the mind of God, as manifested throughout history in his dealings with men and women. Therefore, in reading Scripture, one must search for two intended meanings: *the intended meaning of the author* for his time and place, and *the intended meaning of God* for all times and places.

Before taking each of these in turn, the reader should remember this distinction: The intended meaning is neither the stripped-down, demythologized, bare literal meaning nor a purely figurative meaning over which the imagination can run wild. It is something in between the two. At the one extreme, the purely academic Scripture scholar can get to the literal meaning, whether he or she believes Jesus is Lord or not. At the other extreme, the wild-eyed Christian enthusiast can wax poetic and draw all kinds of figurative conclusions that are light years away from what the writer intended ("Even the devil can quote Scripture to prove a point"; "My opinion's as good as anybody else's!" etc.). But only the mind and heart and spirit of the balanced believer can penetrate to what the author and his Inspirer really meant.

WHAT THE AUTHOR INTENDED

Very few people claim to be able to understand a mathematics book, especially after the first reading. It's filled with all those funny symbols, and most of us just don't know the code well enough to give any opinion of the book at all. Similarly, most of us can't read through a physics text and say, "This book stinks!" We just don't know enough about the subject and the language to have a worthwhile opinion. And yet I'd be rich if I had a dollar for every time one of my high school students finished a Shakespeare play or a Chesterton essay or an Eliot poem and said, "That stunk!"

What they mean, of course, is not that the book gives off an odor but that they found it unpleasant. It had nothing to say to them. But they rarely go farther and ask *why* it had nothing to say to them. In fact, what they are really—and illegitimately—saying is that, because it had nothing to say to *them*, it had nothing to say at all. The cause for this, I think, is that those books are written in English; most of the words they'd seen before, but the thing still doesn't make sense. And if the book doesn't make sense, since it's in a language they've all spoken since childhood, the fault must be with the book and not with them. The trouble is that Shakespeare and Chesterton and Eliot—and the Bible—are more high-powered than their readers. They use language and logic on a higher level than the reader has been prepared for. But, like the fox in the fable, if such readers can't reach them, the grapes must be sour. According to *The Jerome Biblical Commentary:*

> *Because scripture is inspired and presumably this inspiration was for the good of all, there has arisen the fallacy that everyone should be able to pick up the Bible and read it profitably. If this implies that everyone should be able to find out what the sacred author is saying without preparation or study, it really demands of God in each instance a miraculous dispensation from the limitations imposed by differences of time and circumstance.*

In the books mentioned above, including the Bible, the author's period of time, manner of expression, and cast of thought are so far removed from our own that his books are as complicated as a math book and a physics book. His primary obligation was to be intelligent to people of his own times. And yet, in each case, he does have something to say to our times too, provided we are willing to give him more effort than it takes to read the sports pages or a romantic novel. In order for a person to read the Bible with intelligent appreciation, one's scriptural education should be proportionate to

his or her general education. That's why this present book was written, to make at least a beginning at forming an ability to enter that treasury.

To find out what a passage of Scripture meant when it was written, one has to look at two things: (1) the literary form of the passage and (2) the meaning of the passage in the particular author's overall plan.

The first question is the literary form. Is the author at this point speaking literally or figuratively? For instance, if he refers to Jerusalem, does he mean it as the actual city or as a symbol for the Church (the new Israel) or for heaven (the City of God)? Or all three? When you know that in the Book of Daniel, say, the author is secretly writing a series of short stories about a contemporary king, and not recording the actual history of a long-dead one, you begin to understand that he didn't necessarily claim to have seen four beasts with eyes and wings all over them. You begin to realize that the authors of the New Testament are not to be judged by the criteria of strict historical method but by the criteria of truthful preaching and teaching. If one admits that a certain part of the Scripture is fiction, he or she is not denying its historicity—because it was never meant to be history. Biblical fiction is just as inspired and just as true as biblical history.

The second question is the place of this section in the author's overall plan. There is a special problem in biblical study because of the long history of editing, interpreting, and reinterpreting pieces of material over and over again. What has this author done to the material handed on to him? As we have seen, the books of the New Testament were the result of a *process*: they were not written by one man but by a whole series of men, and each was inspired to see some different facet as he reworked the material and passed it on.

When Mark wrote to his Roman pagan converts and Matthew wrote to his Jewish converts, they had two very different audiences. The two men had the same basic intention and message, but the parts of their gospels—even those dealing with the same event—are given a different coloration because of the differing interests and receptivities of their audiences. As we will see comparing the same events in Mark, Matthew, and Luke, the individual author's theological intention in each passage comes clear in the way he adapts material common to all three.

(1)Therefore, to find the author's intended meaning, one must first see what literary form he uses to get this idea across and then (2) how this particular event has been adapted and edited by this particular author. The first question is the subject of form criticism, and the second question is the

subject of redaction (editing) criticism. For answers to these two questions on any particular passage of the Bible, one can look in *The Jerome Biblical Commentary* or any similar work.

WHAT GOD INTENDED

Each individual writer in the Scriptures was writing to his own people, at a particular time, about particular problems. But his writing also fits into the whole overall sweep and perspective of the two Testaments—the whole historic pattern of God's relationship with people. This author's communication has a particular meaning at a particular time, but seen against this longer perspective of God's consistent pattern of fidelity, what the author says takes on an even richer meaning. We have seen this when we dealt with the Old Testament prophets. They did not see photographically into the distant future, but, unbeknownst to them, God used their writings to prepare for the future. When Isaiah saw Israel as the suffering servant of God, he did not see a young carpenter-rabbi hauling his cross up to Calvary. What he saw was his countrymen suffering for their faith, and he urged them to see that Yahweh had always rewarded that faith. But, seen in the whole history of God's dealings with the faithful, including his dealings through Jesus with the New Israel, Isaiah's vision has even deeper meanings than he could have known.

How can a writer write a piece of work which has meanings that even he doesn't know? Let me give you an example. When I wrote the script for a play called *Tender Is the Knight,* I intended it to be a satire on education, on people being trained to combat the ideas of people they have never even met. The knights trained to kill dragons and the dragons trained to kill knights sheerly on the basis of propaganda, without ever asking themselves whether they really wanted to kill their so-called opposition or even whether the opposition deserved to be killed. I had intended it to be a gentle poke at my own theological training, and was half-tempted to call the dragons names like "Luther" and "Calvin." But when the show was over, people were asking me if it was a satire on war. Others wondered if it were a satire on racial prejudice. I hadn't been thinking of those idiocies when I wrote it, but I had to admit—after the fact—that what I had said was true of those human activities as well as of any kind of witless antagonism based on uncritical use of propaganda. Similarly, later members of the Church could see implications in the gospels which the original writers may not have purposely put there.

What, then, are the criteria by which a reader can tell that he or she has more or less gotten the meaning God intended—over and above the intentions of the individual writer?

First of all, this larger sense has to be a legitimate development of the author's intended meaning—as it was with the further insights into *Tender Is the Knight*. It must be a fuller understanding of the original and not merely a wrenching of the original. When modern fundamentalists see the Antichrist in the book of Revelation as a foreshadowing of Hitler or Napoleon or the Roman papacy, they are seeing something far different from the writer's intention. When St. Augustine turns the parable of the Good Samaritan into an allegory of the fall of man, he is wrenching the author's text far from the author's intention. When a modern preacher sees the widespread paganism and materialism in today's world as a parallel to Israel's whoring after idols or when he sees the starving of the world as the man beaten by the roadside and the capitalist nations as the priest and levite, he is legitimately applying the author's meaning to a situation the author could never have envisioned. In this way, the Scripture truly is God's Word for *all* time, even though it was written by men of the first century for men and women of the first century.

Secondly, it is wise to know something about the whole Bible to be sure that the wider meaning one sees actually is a part of a continuing pattern of God's dealings with people. The New Testament writers, inspired by God, see that just as God fed the Israelites with manna, he feeds the New Israel with the Eucharist. They see that what Moses was to Israel, Jesus was to the Christian Church. What Jesus says implicitly about himself becomes explicit when Paul and Acts interpret Jesus' acts and words. Still later, the Church reflects on the Scriptures and evolves even more out of them in the light of ever-expanding human knowledge.

These two criteria aren't always easy to apply, and it's worth being cautious before one stands up and says he or she has a totally new insight into a passage. Those whose knowledge of the Bible is vastly superior to yours or mine are far more hesitant and more willing to submit their theories to the judgment and authority of their peers.

WHAT IS THE MEANING TO ME?

One can get to the author's intended meaning at least on the literary level and know what every scholar in the world has to say about a particular passage and know how this notion has been treated throughout the whole course of Scripture, without his or her life being changed. It is no more than

studying the sources and techniques and dates of Shakespeare's plays. If the Bible is no more than "exam fodder" or a source of proof-texts for debate or an academic dalliance, one's religious convictions and spiritual life will remain unaffected.

In reading Scripture, as in reading Shakespeare, there is a place for both the head and the heart. One can analyze, dissect, probe logical relationships—as a mathematician would—and the text will yield up far more than it ever has before. But, once all the analysis has been done, one must go back and re-read the text with completely different powers of the soul—imagination, emotion, love, spirit, as a poet would. Otherwise, one is left after the analysis with the various parts of a corpse. Analysis reveals hidden parts, but only imagination can re-enliven them.

One can study *Hamlet* line by line, word by word, but the only purpose of that analysis is so that the next time one sees the actual play it will echo even more broadly and profoundly in one's soul. Similarly, one can analyze the Scriptures line by line, word by word, but the only purpose of that analysis is so that the next time one prayerfully re-reads that passage, the risen Jesus shines through the lines even more powerfully and with finer resonances. Both the mathematician and the poet are needed; one without the other is insufficient. Neither the dry demythologizing of the mathematician nor the wild rhapsodizings of the poet will put one in authentic contact with the living Christ.

A purely objective observer of the sayings and events of Scripture— whether he or she was actually there when they happened or whether he or she reads about them 2,000 years later—will never truly find the intended meaning of those books until they are read with the eyes of a believer. The books of the Bible are written from a faith rooted deeply in people's experience of the eternal. Surely, one can get a general idea of what's being said in them if he or she knows the "literary codes." But one will never re-experience them as they were intended and as they were first read until undergoing oneself that same experience of the eternal. When you meet the hero of the gospels for yourself, person-to-person, the gospels become whole new books. But how do we get those who have not met this hero to risk praying? Perhaps we can only tantalize them by the joy of our lives.

2

THE AUTHORS:
DIVINE AND HUMAN

INSPIRATION

In order to face the problems of the author's meaning for his own times and God's meaning for all times in Scripture, we skirted a problem in the last chapter. Is God the author of Scripture (as we have always been told) or is the human author who interprets the message passed on to him also to be considered in some sense the author?

> It was not by the will of man that prophecy arose in former times: rather being impelled by the Holy Spirit, men though they were, they spoke under the agency of God (2 Pet 1:2).

According to this one verse it would seem that the writer of any particular scriptural book was merely carried along by the Spirit of God, like a ship before an irresistible wind. Indeed, some Jewish scholars believed that God somehow "seized" the sacred writer and merely used him as an inert channel, with no personal control or influence over the message he spoke—

---

as a medium is "used" in a seance. Some theologians of the Middle Ages and later believed God must have dictated the books of the Old and New Testaments and, like good secretaries, their "writers" merely copied what they were told, word for word.

These explanations certainly guarantee the absolute authenticity of the Scriptures, but they also leave God open to the charge of now and again mixing up numbers and even occasionally of faulty grammar. What's more, we surely "hear" different personalities coming through in the books of Scripture. It is not just one "homogenized" voice. There is the down-to-earth style of Mark, the elegance of Luke; there is the fiery anger of Jeremiah, the lush eroticism of The Song of Songs.

Furthermore, in the very few times scriptural authors describe their own efforts at writing, it sounds as ordinary and plodding a task as writing any other essay or sermon. They seem to be men who would agree with Red Smith: "Writing's easy; all you have to do is sit at your typewriter till beads of blood form on your forehead!"

> *I shall bring my own work to an end here too. If it is well composed and to the point, that is just what I wanted. If it is trashy and mediocre, that is all I could manage. (2 Macc. 15: 37–38*

> *Seeing that many others have undertaken to draw up accounts of the events that have taken place among us, exactly as these were handed down to us by those who from the outset were eyewitnesses and ministers of the word, I in my turn, after carefully going over the whole story from the beginning, have decided to write an ordered account for you, Theophilus, so that your Excellency may learn how well founded the teaching is that you have received. (Lk 1: 1–4)*

These rare passages when the sacred writer described his own process of composition seem to suggest not only that he made a distinctly individual contribution to the final book, but that it was hard work. Reacting to these statements, other theologians believed that God might have given the writer the thought content of the book but left the choice of words and images to him and that God stepped in only to nudge the writer away from error—the way a good writing teacher or editor would, not doing the actual composition or revision but directing it.

In a sense, we face here a question quite similar to the one about prophecy in the first volume. Did God lift up the prophet, carry him into the

future, and return him to his people with a photographic, literal description of their future? Surely the God who could create a universe from nothing and who is himself free of time and space could have done such a thing. Or did God sit down in the prophet's home, as Genesis pictures him sitting in Abraham's tent, and meticulously map out the future? Or did he give prophets the actual visions they describe—the heavenly court ablaze with Yahweh's power, the sky filled with wheels, etc.?

The obvious use of figurative language and the only approximate relationship of the prophet's "rough map" to the actual historical outcome (also recorded in non-scriptural books) seem to suggest some other method of cooperation between God and the speaker or prophet or writer. Two things, however, seem clear from the evidence: (1) In some very powerful sense, God is the author of Scripture. Throughout the histories of both the Jewish and Christian communities, the sacred books have always been held to be "the word of God." When the New Testament quotes the Old Testament and says, "It is written," the statement which follows becomes unarguable because it is a statement from God. (2) In another sense, the individual writer also has to be considered as an author of his book. It is a result of his labor, the experiences he has had even outside his prayer, the contents of his imagination. His unique personality and views of life definitely "color" the final work—just as a musical melody line is given a recognizably different quality if it is played on a violin or on a tuba.

God is the indirect author of the Scripture, of course, in the sense that, since he is the creator of the world, he is remotely the author of all that takes place in it afterwards. But his influence in the actual writing of Scripture must have been far more direct than that. It is his message, and 2,500 years of believers have treated the Bible as if it were a *direct* communication of his views to them.

One way of dealing with the question is to say that God is the author of the whole Bible and the individual writers are authors merely of the parts. In this view, God is like the architects of the great cathedrals. The architect designed the whole building, but he left the individual artisans to embellish his basic plan with their own scroll work and leaves and gargoyles. Although it is insufficient, this concept does reveal several interesting truths about the Scriptures. The whole word of God is not contained in any single verse of Scripture—nor even in any one book. The at-times sour Ecclesiastes reveals one facet at one time, the sensitive Hosea reveals another facet at another time. Matthew shows characteristics of Jesus which are more meaningful to a Jew; Luke shows characteristics more understandable to a Gentile. The

totality of the Scripture reveals a *pattern* of God's dealings with humanity, first through the Jewish people and then through the Christian people. Overall, however multi-faceted, it is one message and that message is God's, not the individual writer's.

The word used for the relationship between the divine author and the individual human author is called "inspiration." This means not merely a momentary flash of inspiration, like the children in an old movie being struck with the idea, "We could put on a show!" Although inspiration is most intense during the actual process of composition, it is a long-term relationship between God the author and man the author. God has, in a sense, "groomed" the writer for his role through the writer's relationship with the rest of the community of God, for whom he will be the voice. He has "groomed" him also through the writer's study of previous scriptural books, through the influences of his life-experience, through his secular studies, through the qualities of his parents, his teachers, and his whole social and moral environment.

However, the individual completed book is not just a statement about human life as any wise and godly person of that particular time might see it. It is the result of an overwhelming inner conviction of the truth under the influence of God's inspiration. The painter may have carefully prepared his or her tools, but the final work is the creation not of the brushes and paint and canvas but of the artist.

Something remotely similar can be seen in the old cliché of the writer who is indebted to his or her "muse." The writer is not just a passive, static tool in her hands. Rather, the work is the result of a free—and at times even joyous—submission of the artist to the "lead" of his or her inspiration. The author is certain of being led along not just by the natural logical unfolding of the idea itself. Nor is it merely the natural unfolding of ideas and images he or she has ingested in the past. The author is truly "under the influence" of a power higher than himself or herself and *freely* goes along with it. The author truly wants to say what he or she says, but truly contributes his or her own personal skills and experience to the work. And yet the author is certain that the ultimate source of his or her ideas and words is not merely the author.

Like so many realities we have encountered in these pages, the reality of divine inspiration on a human author is "true but beyond literal description." Even the sacred writers themselves could probably have told us no more than what it was like—since we are dealing once again with an experience

only remotely similar to anything we have experienced ourselves. Still, as before, an inadequate approximation is better than no understanding at all.

Some years ago, John Livingston Lowes wrote a book called *The Road to Xanadu*. In it, after scrupulous research into the experience and readings of Samuel Taylor Coleridge, Lowes tried to show the sources of the individual images and symbols in Coleridge's two poems, "The Rime of the Ancient Mariner" and "Xanadu." Lowes formulated a theory which may cast at least a bit of light on what God was taking in hand when he employed a human person as the instrument for proclaiming his message.

Lowes saw the human imagination and memory as a deep well into which all the sense images of one's days and years are dumped. He described the well of the imagination swarming with disconnected sense experiences from all one's ordinary experiences and reading, some still alive and remembered, others long forgotten by the conscious mind: nursery toys, sunsets, the clean smell of grass, poems memorized in childhood, etc. Each of these images is not solitary but, as if like atoms, equipped with "hooks," ready to bond itself onto other images. When a creative idea begins to form at the bottom of this rich well, it boils toward the surface, attracting to itself congenial concrete, sensory images which will most aptly embody the non-physical idea the writer has.

Thus, sensory pictures from Coleridge's reading at one time about the weed-clotted Sargasso Sea off the Bahamas and his reading at another time about St. Elmo's fire and his reading at still another time about theories of the spontaneous generation of small animals all lay ready in his imagination until he needed to describe an eerie, unworldly ship's graveyard to which the Ancient Mariner was condemned:

> *The very deep did rot: O Christ!*
> *That ever this should be!*
> *Yea, slimy things did crawl with legs*
> *Upon the slimy sea.*
>
> *About, about, in reel and rout*
> *the death-fires danced at night;*
> *The water, like a witch's oils,*
> *Burnt green, and blue, and white.*

Perhaps, at the very moment of composition itself, Coleridge did not even realize how he was subconsciously affected by the tone and tempo of the quite similar speeches of the witches in *Macbeth*.

It is this kind of mind and this well of imagination which God prepares in his chosen spokesmen—a whole complex personality, an instrument perfectly attuned to the part of the message he is chosen to speak. It is doubtful whether Isaiah or Mark or Paul ever consciously realized they were writing "Scripture." Rather, each was on fire with the Spirit of God and with the message, the word which that Spirit had conceived in him—just as our Lady, under the movement of that same Spirit, was physically filled with the Word himself.

That last metaphor is perhaps not completely without value. Geneticists and psychologists can study the interaction between the independent male and female factors in the body and personality of a child which is the product of *both* "authors." But they cannot, and probably will not, penetrate the mystery of that cooperation which results in a human person who embodies, in different ways, both parents. Similarly, Scripture scholars and theologians can study the interaction between the divine author and the human authors of Scripture, but they probably will not penetrate the mystery of a cooperation that results in a work which embodies, in different ways, both authors.

Whether in science or in religion, myth—educated guesses, inadequate approximations, fallible symbols—is the only way we can deal with mystery.

WITHOUT ERROR?

The reader of the previous pages will probably not be shocked when I say that I have a lot of trouble with fundamentalists. My problems with such people who take every word and sentence of the Bible as if it were literally true rise principally from my lack of patience (and, alas, charity) for people who zero in on one tree at a time and neglect the rest of the forest, people who treat one sentence as if it were the whole Bible. I have, I confess, a very low tolerance for courageous ignorance. And my problem is not just with staunchly believing fundamentalists but, paradoxically, with staunchly disbelieving fundamentalists.

Believing fundamentalists assail me with, "I won't call priests 'father' because Matthew 23:8 says, 'Call no man "father"'" (They always have the text numbers at their fingertips!) When I ask what they call their own male parents, they pass quickly on to quote Hebrews 2: 3 to prove that all people who cannot bring themselves sincerely to affirm Christ are, *ipso facto*, sinners. Sometimes I try to play their game and ask if they have never sinned with their eyes. When they must admit that they have, I ask, "Why

do you still have both eyes, then, since Matthew 5: 29 says, 'If your eye scandalize you, pluck it out!' " That usually gives them pause, but it is only momentary, and they're off in some other direction, trying to trip me up, trying to show that I am an apostate or at the very least a mealy-mouthed liberal. Their reason, like themselves, is simple: God wrote every verse of the Bible, and therefore every verse of Scripture is without error, and therefore to quibble with any verse is to quibble with (i.e., deny) God.

On the other hand, the non-believing fundamentalist—who is just as myopic—throws up "all those contradictions in the Bible." His or her first tack is scientific. After all, didn't Galileo disprove the whole thing when he proved there was no "firmament" and that the earth isn't the center of the universe? Didn't Darwin shoot down the whole Adam and Eve thing when he proved men came from apes? Didn't Einstein show that the Ascension was impossible? The second task is moral: Where did Cain's wife come from if Eve was the only woman around? Did they commit incest? And what about all those slaughters in the Old Testament where every man, woman, and innocent child were killed "in the name of God"? And the third tack is scholarly (there are only a few of those). In Genesis 7: 17 Noah's flood lasted forty days and in Genesis 7: 24 it lasted a hundred and fifty days. Which was it? And Luke has Jesus ascend on the very day of the Resurrection in his gospel, but in Acts he has him wait around forty more days. Which was it? All of which is supposed to make the Scriptures collapse in disgrace as a flim-flam or a house of cards. "If the Scriptures are supposed to be without error, I've just shown you seven errors! *That* takes care of the Scriptures!"

If you look at Sophocles' play *Oedipus* you can find all kinds of logical inconsistencies. Surely a man like Oedipus, who had already gone to such lengths to escape the curse of marrying his own mother, would never have married—and certainly not a woman at least fifteen years his senior. Surely Jocaste, his wife-mother, who had pierced and bound the ankles of her son and exposed him on a mountain to avoid the same curse, would have noticed that her new husband had some pretty suspicious scars on his own legs.

There are flaws in the play, but that does not negate it as a powerful and true statement about the nature of man, and it does not keep it from being one of the greatest literary masterpieces of Western literature. In order to begin to understand the major truth about man which Sophocles is probing, one must "suspend one's disbelief." The spectator must also overlook the undeniable fact that the walls of the set are not stone but canvas, that Oedipus does not bleed real blood but red dye, that trivial incongruities of

motivation are secondary to Sophocles' message. It is just so with love: Unless one suspends one's scrutiny of the warts, one will never meet the person behind them. It is just so with the Scriptures.

Much the same type of critic as our non-believing fundamentalist condemns the Church completely because of the undeniable brutality of the Crusades and the Inquisition, the scandalous popes of the Renaissance, the perennial cancer of many Church people's concern for money. But for all its flaws, glaring and trivial, the Church goes on. For all its inconsistencies, the Church still feeds the hungry, clothes the naked, instructs the ignorant. Such critics focus solely on the holes and patches and give not the slightest attention to the whole fabric which surrounds them.

Both the Church and the Scriptures are the human embodiment of a divine Spirit. If there are flaws, the fault is in the human element, not in the divine.

The issues with fundamentalists can be resolved (theoretically, at least!) by considering four clarifications which avoid the fundamentalist's objections while at the same time not compromising the Scriptures' integrity.

(1) As a divine-human document, the Scriptures enjoy not freedom from flaws but freedom from lies. I may try my very best to tell the absolute truth, but that does not make me free of any fear of speaking unclearly. What the sacred writers say about the relationship between God and people is in no way threatened by an occasional slipup or inconsistency here or there. What the Scriptures say is so overwhelmingly right that it would be as juvenile to reject the Bible because it has a few flawed passages as it would be to foreswear the United States because we have had a few flawed Presidents.

(2) Consequently, one must consider the whole Bible, not just a single verse or event. The whole Bible cannot be limited on any question to one single stage in the development of revelation. Of course *herem*—the wholesale slaughter of conquered peoples—is condemned over and over again by the same Bible which seems at one time to have called for it. The same gospel which seems to give privileged place to the poor also shows Jesus dining with and evangelizing the rich. The same Lord is both the Lamb of God and the Lion of Judah. Many times Jesus himself "corrects" (i.e., brings to final development) statements of the Old Testament when he says, "You have heard it said . . . but *I* say to you . . ." To make one verse equal the whole message of Scripture is like condemning a person who has always led an exemplary life because he or she has made one single, stupid mistake.

(3) One must also be careful to judge the intention of an author's statement by the *form* which he uses to put the statement forward. Strict

fundamentalists are stuck with defending as literally true the existence of serpents who talked and whales who dutifully acted as vehicles. One is freed from such difficulties by admitting that myth and symbolic stories cannot be judged by the same norms as literal statements—but they nonetheless embody *truth*. As Vatican Council II declared:

> *Those who search out the intention of the sacred writers must, among other things, have regard for "literary forms." For truth is proposed and expressed in a variety of ways, depending on whether its form is that of prophecy, poetry, or some other type of speech.* De Revelatione, 3: 12

(4) Finally, the fundamentalist must realize that God's message of salvation is *the* purpose of Scripture. God is not teaching cosmology or geography or the natural sciences. He was not ripping off pages of the calendar for Moses or Jesus. He was not inventing new geologies for the flood or for the Red Sea. Whatever the methods of communication used in various parts of the Bible, they are all trying to embody one truth, the truth Jesus embodied: God is with us.

In the end, faced with the questions of inspiration and inerrancy in the Bible, we are brought back once again to figurative language. It is interesting to notice that the Latin roots of the words for "breathe" (*spirare*) and "spirit" (*spiritus*) are the same. It is interesting also to realize that the word "to inspire" is exactly the same (*inspirare*), "to breathe into." The earliest theologians of the Church referred to the books of Scripture as *theopneustos*, "God-breathed." This is the same image of enlivening breath which the author of Genesis uses at the creation of the world when he speaks of the "wind of God" or "God's spirit" hovering over the formless void. It is the same image he uses at the creation of man when God "breathed into his nostrils a breath of life, and thus man became a living being." It is the same Holy Spirit, the power of God who overshadowed our Lady and enlivened in her Jesus, the Word of God. It is the same Spirit whom Acts pictures "like a powerful wind from heaven" when the young Church was enlivened to rise and face the world with the Word.

Christ and the Church and the Scriptures—all embody, physicalize, concretize the Spirit and the aliveness of God. The inspiration—the breathing-in—of that Spirit into Jesus and the Christian community and its writings is as mysterious and ultimately unexplainable as the mystery of life itself. All scientific and scholarly attempts fall short, just as all imaginative and poetic attempts fall short. Both the scholars and the poets who wrote Scripture were

attempting the impossible: to encase the reality of God in words. But even a glimmer of that light is better than the darkness.

In no better—and no worse—a way than an academic scripture scholar, Gerard Manley Hopkins, S.J., stood in inarticulate awe before that Spirit who enlivened Jesus and the Church and the Scripture:

> *Oh, morning, at the brown brink eastward, springs—*
> *Because the Holy Ghost over the bent*
> *World broods with warm breast and with ah! bright wings.*

Who can say whether the Scripture scholar with his or her knowledge of languages and Near-Eastern literatures comes any closer than the black poet and preacher James Weldon Johnson? In his human, and therefore—by definition—flawed, way he captured something of the movement of God among people when he wrote:

> *Up from the bed of the river*
> *God scooped the clay;*
> *And by the bank of the river*
> *He kneeled him down;*
> *And there the great God Almighty*
> *Who lit the sun and fixed it in the sky,*
> *Who flung the stars to the most far corner of the night,*
> *Who rounded the earth in the middle of his hand;*
> *This great God,*
> *Like a mammy bending over her baby,*
> *Kneeled down in the dust*
> *Toiling over a lump of clay*
> *Till he shaped it in his own image;*
>
> *Then into it he blew the breath of life,*
> *And man became a living soul.*
> *Amen. Amen.*

3

THE SEED:
JESUS' LIFE
AND MESSAGE

The presupposition of the whole New Testament is the historical Jesus—and actual, living, breathing human being. If he had not proclaimed his message of the kingdom of God to the people of his time in Palestine, there never would have been a Christian church or a Christian testament. Like-wise, if he had not been executed as a dangerous revolutionary and if his friends had not been absolutely convinced that he had risen from the dead, there never would have been a Paul or Mark or Matthew or Luke or John. Without the historical Jesus, those men would have existed, but their names would have been forgotten forever.

But the early Church felt free to add to the words of Christ, to fabricate events and words and describe Jesus as doing them and saying them—in order to show their audiences how Jesus would have handled their current problems consistently with his message. And so it is difficult to peel away the layers of additions and find the core of the gospel which is indisputably the

words and deeds of this historical Jesus. (Even more so for an audience unfamiliar with the Greek language in which the New Testament was first written.)

This excavation process is made even more complicated. Although the disciples mentioned in the gospels actually touched the historical man, Jesus, before his death, they—and even more so their disciples—were far more interested in the risen Lord, whom they knew was still living in their midst and whom they trusted would come soon on the clouds of heaven. In a sense, the historical Jesus was no more; only the historic Jesus was important for them now. Paul, for instance, says nearly nothing about the events of Jesus' life and instead speaks almost exclusively in his letters about the Crucifixion and Resurrection: the core of the gospel message. What happened beforehand was completely secondary to the cataclysmic news about the Resurrection. Linguistically, the accounts of the Passion and Resurrection are the oldest sections, the core of the gospel. In a very true sense, the final editions of the gospels are little more than "the Passion with very long introductions." Furthermore, when the early community and then the evangelists fabricated stories about Jesus dealing with problems of their later times and presented them as if Jesus had dealt with those problems in his time, they felt the process was perfectly legitimate. After all, the risen Jesus *was* actually in their presence, conducting his ministry through them, and inspiring them to come up with answers consistent with his basic, historical message.

A third problem which we will see in more detail in the rest of these pages is that each evangelist, in setting up the structural outline of his gospel, was more interested in developing doctrine than in writing a chronological history. Matthew, for instance, sets up his structure on five great sermons in preparation for the Passion—to parallel the five great books of the Hebrew Scriptures. Luke, on the other hand, structures his gospel on one, and only one, gradual journey to Jerusalem—in order to climax the movement of the Church in the formerly focal city of God's plan and then, in Acts, to show the movement of the Church from Jerusalem (and therefore from Judaism) to the new focal city of God's plan, Rome—the center of the whole known world. The question of particular times of occurrence and particular settings is completely secondary to their theological development. Therefore, the outlines of the four gospels are of little value in setting forth the strict historical progress of Jesus' life.

To sum up, then: There are three basic problems in unearthing the

authentic, historical Jesus from the New Testament: (1) the additions and amplifications made by the early Church, (2) their primary concern with the present, living, risen Lord rather than with the historical Jesus, and (3) the evangelists' primary concerns with theological development rather than with accurate chronological development.

However, with scientific philological techniques too complex to go into here, biblical scholars have been able to peel away the various layers of additons by studying linguistic and cultural differences. Like all good scientists, they disagree, and they always advance their conclusions as theories and not facts. But there is a large body of data concerning Jesus about which all competent scholars agree. The means by which they arrive at their conclusions and consensus are way beyond the beginner, but I will try in these pages to simplify them without falsifying them. For those with a little acquaintance with Greek, a book like Perrin's can take them even farther.

JEWS IN PALESTINE IN JESUS' TIME

Jesus lived in occupied territory, subject to Romans, whom Jews considered godless Gentiles. It was a territory sacred to them as the people of God and sacred to God as the land from which he would save mankind. His countrymen believed it was an abomination in the sight of God that these pagans should have control over this holy land and its holy temple, and they believed that God would soon step in himself and remedy matters.

But, as it always had been, the task of the people was to be the agents of Yahweh's will. Consequently, various sects grew up, differing among themselves as to the best way to help things along. The *Zealots* were extremists, not unlike the Zionists of thirty years ago who finally did regain Israel by means of underground warfare and guerilla armies. The Zealots of Jesus' day were engaged in the same kind of activities and, after his death, these culminated in the unsuccessful war against Rome and the destruction of the temple. Simon, one of Jesus' disciples, and perhaps also Judas Iscariot were "converts" to Jesus from this sect.

Contrary to the one-sided picture of them given in the gospels and even more in sermons, the *Pharisees* were what we might call the "liberals" of first-century Judaism. They held that every aspect of human life was governed by the law, but they realized that no written document can cover every detail of life once and for all. Changing conditions demand a living, flexible code. Therefore, they claimed that the law had to be interpreted and even

amended, just as the Congress and the Supreme Court interpret and amend the United States Constitution. However, they did claim that only Pharisees could legitimately do any of this interpreting.

Against them stood the *Sadducees*. They were both literalist and conservative, which is not an unusual combination. The reason for their caution was that they were few in number but very wealthy and class-conscious. They did not want any trouble with Rome.

A fourth group, the *Essenes*, were even more rigid in their interpretations than the Sadducees. They expected the Day of Yahweh almost immediately and withdrew to secluded desert communes of rigorous obedience and penance in order to prepare themselves for it. This sect is very probably the source of the Dead Sea Scrolls. It is not inconceivable that John the Baptizer was a member of one of these groups.

These mutually antagonistic factions, however, bred a deep division among the people of the Jewish community. Not only did one sect despise all the others, but they despised those in no sect at all, because all the others were making more difficult the job of preparing a pure Israel, worthy of Yahweh's entrance for his battle against the contaminating pagans. When Jesus said that brother would turn against brother and children against their parents, he was talking about a reality.

Especially despised by all four sects were the pariahs and outcasts of the community: "tax collectors and sinners" who were collaborators with the invaders, prostitutes who consorted with the enemy's soldiers, Samaritans whom the Jews detested on grounds of not only racial but religious prejudices, swineherds like the prodigal son who dealt in ritually unclean goods. To the upright Jew such people, increasing Israel's impurity, were delaying the visitation of Yahweh and the liberation of the people. Ironically, it was precisely to these outcasts that Jesus came.

THE LIFE OF JESUS

Let us listen to the words of Norman Perrin:

> We are now in a position to make a general statement about the life of Jesus. He was baptized by John the Baptist, and the beginning of his ministry was in some way linked with that of the Baptist. In his own ministry Jesus was above all the one who proclaimed the Kingdom of God and who challenged his hearers to respond to the reality he was proclaiming. The authority and effectiveness of Jesus as proclaimer of the Kingdom of God

was reinforced by an apparently deserved reputation as an exorcist. In a world that believed in gods, in powers of good and evil, and in demons, he was able, in the name of God and his Kingdom, to help those who believed themselves to be possessed by demons.

A fundamental concern of Jesus was to bring together into a unified group those who responded to his proclamation of the Kingdom of God, irrespective of their sex, previous background or history. A central feature of the life of this group was eating together, sharing a common meal that celebrated their unity in the new relationship with God, which they enjoyed on the basis of their response to Jesus' proclamation of the Kingdom. In this concern for the unity of the group of those who responded to the proclamation, Jesus challenged the tendency of the Jewish community of his day to fragment itself and in the name of God to reject certain of its own members. This aroused deep-rooted opposition to him, which reached a climax during a Passover celebration in Jerusalem when he was arrested, tried by the Jewish authorities on a charge of blasphemy and by the Romans on a charge of sedition, and crucified. During his lifetime he had chosen from among his followers a small group of disciples who had exhibited in their work in his name something of his power and authority.

That, or something very like it, is all that we can know; it is enough.

And after Jesus' life was over, his followers were so convinced that he had indeed risen from the dead and was present within their community that they roved the surface of the known world, spreading the Good News, making explicit what was implicit in Jesus' words and deeds, writing letters and versions of the amplified message, suffering persecution and even death rather than deny the Good News, and founding a Christian community which has embodied and evolved the message for nearly 2,000 years.

This is a version of the life of Jesus and its effect on his disciples with which the most skeptical Scripture scholar would probably not quibble. It is more or less certain that all the data in the above extract are historical. What of the other details? Were there angels and shepherds and Magi? Was Jesus betrayed by one of his own men and did he have a private audience with the Roman procurator? Are these details actual and historical or mythic and historic? Each one must be judged on its own merits and a decision made (1) whether this event actually happened as it is described, (2) whether the core of an actual event did occur but was further amplified, (3) whether the event was fabricated to show how Jesus would have handled a later problem, or (4) whether the event was a legendary story which the commu-

nity adopted and "baptized" in order to bring out a further facet of the basic message. This book is only the merest beginning of that task.

THE MESSAGE OF JESUS

What follows is not the only content of the actual message of Jesus which we can arrive at by intensive linguistic study of the New Testament. Very many scholars would assert strongly that there is far more material we can certainly trace back to the mouth of the historical Jesus. The material treated here represents what all competent scholars would generally agree is surely the absolute words of Jesus. How they arrive at these conclusions and at their consensus is, as I have said, far too technical to go into here, but their very credentials and the very fact of their consensus make these scholars trustworthy.

Proclamation of the Kingdom

Four sayings about the Kingdom of God have strong claim to complete authenticity:

> *The time is fulfilled, and the kingdom of God is at hand. (Mk. 1:15a)*
>
> *But if it is by the finger of God that I cast out demons, then the Kingdom of God has come upon you. (Lk. 11:20)*
>
> *The Kingdom of God is not coming with signs to be observed; nor will they say, "Lo, here it is!" or "There!", for behold, the Kingdom of God is in the midst of you. (Lk. 17:20–21)*
>
> *From the days of John the Baptist until now, the Kingdom of Heaven has suffered violence, and men of violence plunder it. (Matt. 11:12)*

The theme of the "kingdom of God"—"kingdom of Heaven"—"eternal life" is *the* central message of Jesus. No matter what additions or explicitations the later community made, this was the core of his preaching. But what does he mean by those three interchangeable terms? "Kingdom" is an apocalyptic symbol used by Jewish writers for centuries, picturing Yahweh as a king coming at the head of his celestial armies to rescue and redeem his people and give them a totally new world. But what is the *intended* meaning under that figurative description?

Surely no king visibly and literally appeared on the clouds of heaven. Therefore, the reality he was describing as the "new kingdom" was a

symbol for a reality which was real but not tangible—which is what symbols are for. Did he mean, then, that (a) this kingdom, this eternal life, was something still in the distant future or (b) this kingdom, this eternal life, was something that somehow had already begun and could be experienced in the present?

In the first of the four texts quoted above, the time of preparation seems to be over, but the kingdom itself is still "at hand," i.e., about to begin but not yet begun. By this he could mean something in the distant future or something in the near future. Since scholars agree that this was a statement of the historical Jesus, actually made before his death and resurrection, I personally tend to think that he was probably not speaking of the end of the world but of the kingdom that would be inaugurated at the time of his resurrection and the coming of the Holy Spirit into the new people. However, the phrase here could well mean the fulfillment of the kingdom at the end rather than its inauguration.

The other three, also spoken by the historical Jesus before his death and resurrection, all claim that the kingdom is already present. It "has come." It is "in the midst of you." It has already "suffered violence" by the attacks on John the Baptist, its forerunner, and will continue to suffer violence in the inevitable attack on Jesus himself and in the persecutions his followers will undergo.

Therefore, there seem to be *two* meanings to the coming of the kingdom, one in the present and one in the near (or distant) future. But this does not seem an insurmountable tension. What Jesus seems to be claiming is that the kingdom, eternal life, *is* present here and now, but only in a rudimentary stage which will come to birth in his Resurrection and come to fulfillment in the day of the Lord. It is like a seed which actually exists here and now but does not really reach fulfillment until it is buried (at the Crucifixion), breaks through the earth into new life (the Resurrection), and begins to grow in this new form (the Christian community), to its full maturity (the fully realized Body of Christ in "heaven"). This interpretation seems to me eminently justifiable as the meaning Jesus *intended*, especially when taken in connection with the many, many times in the parables when Jesus himself compares the kingdom to a seed. "Unless the seed fall into the ground and die, it cannot have eternal life."

One interpretation which the third quotation above (Luke 17:20-21) seems to rule out is that the kingdom would be a literal, observable fulfillment of the physical details given in the Jewish and Christian apocalyptic writers. No one will be able to say, "Lo, here it is!" No one should wait to

see a literal, observable change in the world, much less cock his or her ear for trumpet blasts from the sky. Jesus categorically refused to give such a physical sign. The coming of the kingdom, of eternal life, would not be a physical, historical event in the way that a king's getting off a barge or a war between two armies are physical, historical events. The kingdom, eternal life, is not in "signs to be observed," Jesus says; it is rather "in the midst of you." *It is not real in the sense kings and armies are real; it is real in the sense that an inner change in one's entire self is real.*

Jesus' Parables

Almost beyond dispute, the core of each of the New Testament parables can be traced back to Jesus himself. In their original forms, however, they were probably in different settings from the ones given them in the gospels and probably without the point-by-point explanations many of them are given, when the evangelists have Jesus go off alone with the apostles and explain each detail.

The original parables were actually riddles to be unlocked by the individual listener. It was a teaching trick rabbis often used, a trick which is also used by Zen masters half the world away. The Zen master will give his pupil a *koan* and, in unlocking the secret of his *koan*, the pupil will find enlightenment. One of the best known is: "We know the sound of two hands clapping; what is the sound of one hand clapping?"

Similarly, the rabbi—in this case Jesus—gave his disciples riddles in the form of stories. The whole point of the story rested on the fact that its central assertion was, at first hearing, unthinkable, contradictory, impossible. For instance, as we saw earlier in the parable of the Good Samaritan, the basic story is really just a tale about neighborliness. But what puts the twist into it is that the victim is a Jew and the rescuer is a Samaritan. What Jesus was asking his audience to do was wrestle with something they considered impossible: the combination of "good" and "Samaritan."

This call to inner wrestling is lost to us, first of all, because most of us don't have any feelings one way or the other about Samaritans. Perhaps if a member of the John Birch Society could read it as the parable of the "good Communist" or a black person could read it as the parable of the "good Klansman," the impossibility of the combination in Jesus' parable might come clear.

The literal point of Jesus' parables was intended to make his hearers *either* reject the "unthinkable" assertion out of hand or begin to question all

that he has taken for granted about Samaritans. Thus on the literal level it points to an unfair prejudice about Samaritans; it is a call to a social virtue: tolerance. But all symbols not only mean what they say themselves but also point beyond themselves. Here, too, as in all the statements of Jesus, he is making a point about the kingdom. The symbolic point of the story is that the kingdom of God breaks abruptly into a person's consciousness and demands the "overturn of prior values, closed options, set judgments, and established conclusions" (Perrin, p. 293). That's what the kingdom *is*: a total *metanoia* of one's life, a 180° turn from the values of competition, self-protection, cliquishness, and materialism which Jesus' audience—then and now—have blindly accepted from "the world." Even more deeply, it is a total turnabout from our sense of being second-rate, negligible, worthless. It proclaims that we have indeed been adopted—through Jesus—as the sons and daughters of the Most High God.

This theme of the kingdom as a *reversal of one's previous values* is a major theme of many of Jesus' parables. In "the rich man and Lazarus" he uses another symbolic story to make the same point. On earth, the rich man feasted away his days, heedless of Lazarus, the poor leper begging at his gate. This is the way the world sees values. But after death, when the real values come clear, Lazarus is "in the bosom of Abraham" and Dives is tormented in hell. This is "the real reality," exactly counter to the world's idea of reality. This is the kingdom, present among us now, even though worldly prejudices blind us to it.

Therefore, the parables of Jesus are asking us to acknowledge the "real reality" which is the kingdom. But he is also asking us to *do* something about it after we have recognized it. As T. W. Manson put it, "Salvation may be free, but it is not cheap." In parables like "the treasure hidden in the field" and "the pearl of great price," Jesus is saying that, once you have found the treasure and the pearl (i.e., the kingdom), you have to sell all you have (all the old desires and prejudices) to go and buy it, and count yourself lucky to do it. The old values, some of them very good in themselves, pale into insignificance compared to the gift being offered. This gospel message, at its roots, is no call to the consoling bosom of a mothering God.

Jesus' Proverbs

Although we have not seen the proverb form so far in this book, it is not a difficult one to understand, expecially since it is so similar to all the other figurative forms we have seen. "A stitch in time saves nine" on the literal

level says that, if you sew a rip in your clothes when it first happens, you will save yourself work in the long run before the rip gets bigger and takes more sewing. On the figurative level, it means that *any* problem is best faced right at the beginning before it gets out of control and requires much more effort to handle. Like the symbol of the fork in the road in "The Road Not Taken," a proverb takes a commonplace, everyday situation and lets it stand for all kinds of similar human situations. However, a proverb compacts the insight into one sentence—and it becomes a proverb because people say "That's so true!" and repeat it down the years. It expresses an insight into the way things are, or should be.

"Leave the dead to bury their own dead" (Lk. 9:60). This is a complete reversal of our accepted ideas of what is truly important. And how can dead people bury other dead people? Hearing that proverb of Jesus, people don't cock their heads and smile and say "That's so true!" As such, it is a riddle, a *koan*, and it challenges the listener to question his or her values at their deepest places within the person.

> "If anyone strikes you on the right cheek, turn to him the other also; and if anyone would sue you and take your coat, let him have your cloak as well; and if anyone forces you to go one mile, go with him two miles" (Matt. 5:39–41).

These three admonitions truly go against the grain. If we were in one of those situations, our first instinct would be "How dare you?" But when Jesus asks us to turn the other cheek, he is not denying that there are times when people must be punished for injuring us—anymore than he was suggesting that corpses should bury one another in the previous proverb. He is asking us to do some pretty fundamental thinking about all our self-protective values.

In the second admonition, one must remember that the coat and cloak were the *only* two pieces of clothing that the Palestinian peasant had. To take the proverb literally would be to leave the poor man utterly naked. But it was not literal nakedness Jesus was calling for; he was asking for symbolic, inner nakedness.

The third admonition refers to the practice whereby Roman soldiers were allowed to press local citizens into service, carrying loads for them, cleaning their boots, and so forth. Like the other two, it is a command of Jesus that is impossible to take literally. To accept it would be to condemn oneself to a lifetime of forced slavery. What he is saying is that the first mile renders to

Caesar what is Caesar's, gives testimony to the realities of the world. But the second mile renders to God what is God's, gives testimony to the really real. The kingdom is not a reality which "makes sense" to a worldling.

> *"If a kingdom is divided against itself, that kingdom cannot stand. And if a house is divided against itself, that house will not be able to stand. And if Satan has risen up against himself and is divided, he cannot stand, but is coming to an end" (Mk. 3:24–26).*

These are three parallel proverbs. The first two are literally true, but they are used only to set up the third parallel: Just as any earthly kingdom which is undermined by opposition will fall, so Satan's kingdom will fall when opposition to it (i.e., the kingdom of God) spreads wide enough.

But is Jesus speaking literally about a personage with horns and a tail sitting on the throne of the world? Or, if we get rid of the trappings of horns and tail, is he even talking about a single individual who sums up all evil in himself? Probalby not. Satan is a *symbol* of all the selfishness in human beings, and his kingdom is "the world" and its way of looking at reality, which we have accepted. But already, in the subversive work of Jesus, inroads have begun on the "kingdom of Satan," and, through his followers, his work will continue to erode the power of selfishness with the power of love. The charge that Jesus is evil is ridiculous; he is "Satan's" enemy and undoing.

Exercise

In view of what has been said here about proverbs, in the following statement (a) what is Jesus *literally* asking of his listeners and (b) what is he *really* asking them, if they want to enter the kingdom? What is he challenging?

1. "Whoever would save his life will lose it, and whoever loses his life for my sake and gospel's will save it." (Mk 8:35)

2. "How hard it will be for those who have riches to enter the Kingdom of God! . . . It is easier for a camel to go through the eye of a needle than for a rich man to enter the Kingdom of God." (Mk 10:23–25)

3. "Everyone who exalts himself will be humbled, and he who humbles himself will be exalted." (Lk 14:11)

4. "No one who puts his hand to the plough and looks back is fit for the kingdom of God." (Lk 9:62)

5. "Whoever does not receive the kingdom of God like a child shall not enter it." (Mk 10:15)

6. "Love your enemies and pray for those who persecute you, so that you may be sons of your Father." (Mt 5:44)

7. "If your eye should cause you to sin, tear it out and throw it away; it is better for you to enter into life with one eye than to have two eyes and be thrown into a hell of fire." (Mt 18:9)

The Our Father

Next to the florid and wordy prayers common among the people of his day, Jesus' prayer to "Our Father" is spartan in its brevity and simplicity. Because of its brevity and therefore the ease of memorizing it, the version of the prayer in Luke is perhaps the closest we can come to words which Jesus certainly spoke himself:

> *Father,*
> *may your name be held holy,*
> *your kingdom come.*
> *Give us each day our daily bread,*
> *and forgive us our sins,*
> *for we ourselves forgive each one who has sinned against us.*
> *And do not put us to the test (Lk 11:2–4).*

For the person who can say the prayer of Jesus, the kingdom has surely come—but only as a seed, a leaven, to work slowly against the kingdom of Satan, the kingdom of selfishness. He asks that his Father help him to keep his body growing with food and his spirit growing with his Father's forgiveness. And, most radical of all, he asks forgiveness only insofar as he forgives others; in so doing, he flies in the face of the world's values—vindictiveness, getting one's due—by living the kingdom's value—love.

In his novels, C. S. Lewis retells this Christian myth of the "war" between the two kingdoms in completely different symbols. Instead of Satan, he has a committee of rationalistic scientists, business people, and politicans. In place of Jesus, he has Maleldil, the great lord of "deep heaven." The symbols chosen are quite different, but the kingdoms and their war are quite the same; the kingdom of selfishness against the kingdom of love. This is, at the core and before any additions and explicitations, *the* message of the historical Jesus.

The order and some of the content of this chapter are merely a simplification of Chapter 12 of Perrin's book, *The New Testament: An Introduction,* which is an excellent book but written for a more sophisticated audience than the audience the present book was written for. *See* also W. D. Davies' *Invitation to the New Testament,* New York, Anchor, 1969.

4

THE GROWING SEED:
THE DEVELOPMENT OF CHRISTIAN THOUGHT

The gospels are unexplainable unless one considers the religious movement, the early Christian community, which gave them birth. The gospels are
not so much a historical outline as a record of the development of Christian
thought. The content of what became solidified in the New Testament was
generated by an evolving community, trying to apply the message of Jesus to
new situations, trying to explicitate what Jesus had declared only implicitly,
trying to defend itself against attack by Jews and persecution by Gentiles.
The evolution described in this chapter is not as hard-and-fast as the section
headings would suggest. All the stages existed alongside one another and
influenced one another. But it is helpful to see the variety of influences that
the early community underwent on its way from Jerusalem to Rome, from a
sect within Judaism to an independent religion with a worldwide mission.
Further, since Paul did not put dates on his letters, and since the early
Church, as we have said, was not interested in the accuracy of dates and

places, the dates given must always be taken as approximate. However, if the gospels are a product of an evolutionary process, it is helpful to see even an approximate picture of that development.

THE FIRST YEARS:
JEWISH CHRISTIANS IN PALESTINE

The first Christians were Jews. And they were still Jews not merely as citizens but in their religious lives as well. They still attended services in the temple and still kept all the details of the Jewish law, even after the Resurrection. They were a sect of Judaism, just like the Pharisees, the Sadducees, the Essenes, and the Zealots. They believed in the same Yahweh and revered the same Scriptures. The only difference between them and their Jewish brethren was that they claimed Jesus was the Messiah and believed that this claim had been validated by the Resurrection. This, in turn, was a direct attack on the privileged place of the law and the temple. But that was more than enough to make them apostates to their fellow Jews.

All Jews, whether Hebrews or Christians, lived in the same occupied country. Many took the apocalyptic details of the Hebrew prophets like Daniel with a great deal of literalness, and they awaited the literal arrival of a messiah who would be a king like David and a prophet-lawgiver like Moses. Till that time, Hebrews and Hebrew-Christians alike tried to prove themselves worthy of that liberation by scrupulous obedience to the Mosaic law.

Since we have no writings from those first twenty years which have not been incorporated into later works like the gospels, we can only speculate from the linguistic "layers" and varying styles of the New Testament what the particular interests of that first network of communities were. It seems that the community in Jerusalem itself was particularly conservative, legalistic, and accepted as authoritative by its satellite communities. This conservativism could have been motivated, at least in part, by the fact that Jerusalem was the focus of the Jewish religion and therefore the place where Christians were forced to explain themselves in terms the pharisaic mind could understand.

It is safe to suspect that they had at least two purposes in their initial development of the core gospel message: (1) to spread the Good News to their reluctant neighbors and explain what it meant, and (2) to defend themselves when they were hauled before the "sanhedrins and synagogues." One of those persecutors was, by his own admission, Saul of Tarsus who stood by while Stephen, the first martyr, was stoned to death for his "heresies."

After the basic proclamation of the Good News that the kingdom had indeed begun, one of their first tasks was to explain to skeptical and hostile people why the expected Messiah had suffered such a degrading death. To do so, they combed the Hebrew Scriptures—which both orthodox Jews and Christians revered—to show how Jesus had been and still was the fulfillment of God's constant dealings with Israel as his suffering servant. Also, they were at pains to explain the special table fellowship they had had together in the community since the days of Jesus: the Eucharist. Appealing· again to their common heritage, they argued that it was the fulfillment of the Passover supper wherein Jews celebrated their release from bondage in Egypt and their inauguration as the people of God. But the Christian meal was not celebrating their physical release from the Romans (as the Passover celebrated the physical release from the Egyptians); it celebrated their release, within themselves, from the values of the kingdom of the world.

By scientific linguistic techniques, scholars can isolate within our present texts of the Greek New Testament, forms and styles which go back to the very earliest days of the Church. All scholars will agree that, deep below the additions by later writers, there is a body of statements traceable back to the very first years. For short, they call this "sayings source" Q (from the German, *Quelle*, "Source"). Within a few years of the resurrection of Jesus, this was probably already written in a scroll or booklet. It contained, in no more than two hundred or so verses, sayings and stories of Jesus, preserved in his own language and only later translated into Greek. Some were historical; some probably were fabricated to apply his message to later problems. We will see more of Q in the next chapter, since its contents are threaded here and there throughout the gospel versions of Matthew and Luke.

Isolating these earlier linguistic elements in our present gospels, scholars find that the general tone of the Q sayings and stories is dominated by a concern about the nearness of the end. Also, since the only potential converts at the moment were their fellow Jews, much of Q is concerned with explaining the meaning of the message of the kingdom as it was connected with the Hebrew Scriptures, showing that—like Isaiah, Jeremiah, Daniel— Jesus was a prophet interpreting history in the name of God and that his prophetic Spirit lived on in the Christian community. According to F. C. Grant, this very early "gospel before the gospels" contained more or less the following:

The ministry and message of John the Baptizer.

The temptation of Jesus.

The Sermon on the Mount.

The mission of the twelve.

Jesus' teaching about prayer and the Our Father.

Various controversies with the Scribes and Pharisees, especially the charge of relation to Beelzebub.

Jesus' teaching about discipleship:

> freedom from care,
> watchfulness,
> the kingdom as a treasure,
> parables of the mustard seed and the yeast, the great supper
> against self-exaltation.

Sayings about the law and forgiveness.

Sayings about the Second Coming and the parable of the entrusted talents.

This list does not claim that Q contained these ideas in the *form* in which they are presently found in the gospels, but only that, within a few years of the beginning, the seed was there.

When Caligula became emperor in Rome (37–41), he was first hailed by the Jews, but after eighteen months in power, he ordered that he himself be worshiped as a god and that his image should be set up in all places of worship, even in synagogues. When a group of Jews destroyed a small shrine to Caligula in Palestine, the emperor retaliated by commanding that a colossal statue of himself be erected in the Jerusalem temple. When it was delayed, Caligula ordered the governor, Petronius, to commit suicide. Finally, this explosive issue was resolved in 41 A.D. when Caligula was murdered. But the incident is reflected later in the gospels (in terms borrowed from Daniel) when they speak of the presence of "the desolating abomination" in the temple. This, like the later destruction of the temple, they mistook as one of the literal fulfillments of the signs which would herald the end.

THE MISSION TO JEWISH CONVERTS OUTSIDE PALESTINE

The greatest developments in the message came when the early community took the Good News to the "outside world." And that world was *Hellenistic*.

"Hellenism"—from the Greek word *Hellas*, "Greece"—is the name given to the civilization created and spread by the conquests of Alexander

the Great (331–323 B.C.). As he conquered the whole known world of his time, from the Greek peninusla to India and from North Africa to Persia, he and his men brought with them the ideas and customs and language of Greece. Everywhere Greek culture was imitated, and every people spoke Greek, even Palestinian Jews. The effect of having this common language increased enormously the possibility of interchanging ideas, with the result that, while every culture became Hellenized, even Palestinian Judaism, each culture also gave its own coloration to Hellenism as it spread farther and farther with the expansion of the new world empire, Rome.

The Roman conquest did not change the cultural situation very much, since Romans derived their culture from Greece. Only in the second century A.D. did Latin spread eastward from the West and split the world into a Latin world centered in Rome and a Greek world centered in Byzantium.

Jews were scattered throughout this Hellentistic world which was rich with conflicting faiths and philosophies. In part they were descendants of the victims of former catastrophes like the exile into Babylon. But they were also venturesome people who had emigrated from the poverty and parochialism of Palestine. These Jews were bilingual, thinking and speaking easily in both Greek and Aramaic. They translated their Hebrew Scriptures into Greek (*The Septuagint*) and built synagogues in each city where they lived so that they could worship Yahweh, even though they could not worship him "properly" in the temple at Jerusalem.

Palestinian Jews mildy distrusted Hellenistic Jews because they often seemed to be adopting "foreign ways". As a result, when the Jewish persecutions of those Jews who had converted to Christianity became stronger, the Jewish officials were far more tolerant of the Palestinian Jewish Christians than of the Hellenistic Jewish Christians.

Outside Palestine, Hellenistic Jews made their own contributions to Hellenism besides being affected by it. Many Gentiles, upset by the numberless "gods" and the vices of their times, were attracted by the monotheism and the moral code of Judaism. Some were fully converted, accepting even circumcision late in life and the full Jewish dietary laws. Others, although eager to share the Judaic way of life and worship, were understandably not as eager for circumcision and the strictures of Jewish ritual law. These were sufficiently numerous that the Hellenistic Jews coined a name for them: "the God-fearers." As the Christian Jews emerged from Palestine to share the Good News with their Hellenistic Jewish brethren, they found fertile ground for the seed in these "God-fearers." Christianity appealed to such people because they were not forced to be circumcised, while at the same time

participating fully in all that Judaism had to offer—and more. The story of this missionary movement to spread the gospel from Palestine to the outside world was later written in the Acts of the Apostles. The speeches it records are typical examples of Christian preaching in synagogues, to "God-fearers," and on the streets of Greek cities around the Mediterranean. It was these preachers, familiar with the *Septuagint* translation of "Yahweh" (*kurios,* "Lord"), who summed up their message in the single sentence: "Jesus is Lord."

GENTILE CHRISTIANS

Just as God had prepared the Hebrews for the Good News by the evolving ideas given them by the prophets of the Old Testament, he also prepared the Gentiles outside Palestine by the evolving ideas of the Hellenic thinkers and philosophers—Socrates, Plato, Aristotle, the Stoics, the mystery cults. The Greeks thought more naturally of redemption *from* the world rather than transformation *of* the world. They thought more naturally of the immortality of the soul than of the resurrection of the body. But the idea of an other-worldly, heroic redeemer, the conflict between flesh and spirit, the pentecostal gifts of the Spirit in Christianity were something they could understand very well. As the Christian community grew outward from Palestine, it was more and more toward these well disposed Gentiles that the New Testament writers turned in their attempt to "translate" the message into terms and categories that the non-Jewish mind could comprehend.

Moreover, the authors of the epistles and gospels took great pains to ensure that their pagan audiences did not think that Jesus was "just one more god" or that Christianity was just one more mystery cult from the East. Paul, for instance, is insistent in his letters to the Corinthians that they control their wild enthusiasm in such activities as speaking in tongues and the like, lest their faith deteriorate into pseudo-religious orgies. Mark in his gospel strongly argues against the assertion that Jesus is merely one more "divinized man," like Hercules, who had been raised as a reward for his labors to the level of a god or demi-god because he found favor with the gods of Olympus. Mark takes great pains to distinguish Jesus from one of these "divine men." The Christian community was more than willing to be enriched by the new points of view and insights of Gentile converts, but it was strongly unwilling to be diluted by them.

As Christianity moved out into the Hellenistic world, which was more sophisticated and varied than the relatively simpler Palestinian culture, the

different expectations and receptivities of this new audience called for adaptations of methods in preaching to them. Unlike the stories and sayings of the Q document which served the Palestinian communities, the letters of Paul to the missionary churches take the form of general Christian instruction—not stories and sayings of Jesus but theological reflections on the implications of the core kingdom message. Whereas the early community had done this (and still continued to do it) by fabricating stories about Jesus to show how he would have applied the message to a later problem, Paul forthrightly proclaimed his interpretation with far fewer mythic devices. There is very little interest in Paul's letters about the story of the historical Jesus other than in accounts of the founding of the Eucharist, the Passion, and the Resurrection. These letters, which were sent originally to particular communities around the Mediterranean, were later copied and sent elsewhere to be read at eucharistic meetings, since they dealt with characteristic problems Christians faced everywhere in non-Jewish cultures: the relation of pagan Hellenistic forms of religious enthusiasm to the Christian's possession of the Spirit, the relation of the resurrection of Jesus to the future resurrection of the believer, and so on.

One problem for the beginning reader of Scritpure today is to get straight in his or her mind that, although the Acts of Apostles speaks of the history of the early Church and especially of the missionary journeys of Paul, and although it is printed in most Bible versions before the epistles, it was not written until fifteen or twenty years after the events it describes. Moreover, it was written for an audience different from Paul's own, one which had had longer time to reflect and assimilate the original message. Therefore, if one wants to get some idea of the second and third phases of the Church's evolving understanding, he or she can get a better idea from Paul's letters than from Acts. It might help to understand this difference if we considered one event—the Council of Jerusalem—which is treated by both Paul and Acts. Paul discusses it in Galatians (2:1–10), which was written between 50 and 55 A.D. and the same event in Acts (15:1–19), which was written between 70 and 90 A.D.

Paul describes the "Council" between himself and the leaders of the Jerusalem community (Peter, James, John) as resulting from his willingly coming to those eyewitness authorities to submit for their judgment the content of his preaching and his interpretation of the message. Titus, Paul's companion, had not been obliged to be circumcised, and there were present at the meeting several converted Pharisees who insisted that circumcision was essential for Gentile converts. "I was so determined to safeguard you

(Galatians) the true meaning of the Good News, that I refused even out of deference to yield to such people for one moment" (2:5). It was a critical moment, since the result of it would greatly jeopardize the non-Jewish mission. But Paul argued on the grounds of the liberty from the law that Christians enjoy in Christ Jesus, and Peter agreed. Peter would concentrate his efforts more heavily on the conversion of the circumcised (Jews), and Paul would concentrate his on the uncircumcised (Gentiles). It was only later, in Antioch, that Peter and Paul met again, and Paul upbraided Peter for discontinuing his practice of eating with pagans, since Peter was wrongly associating the requirements for being a Christian with the requirements for being a Jew.

This same meeting is also described in Acts, written a generation later for an audience with different problems. The episode falls by design in the middle of the book, because it is the turning point in Luke's story: when the apostolic college at Jerusalem officially recognizes the evangelization of the Gentiles. In this act, the Church officially breaks out of its Jewish womb. As Luke presents it, the council treated two problems: circumcision and the dietary laws, stressing that the authoritative Jerusalem church itself decided it would lay no conditions on Gentile converts. In speeches which Luke consciously makes up and puts on the lips of the speakers, Peter as the first of the disciples settles the circumcision question and James as the head of the Jerusalem community solves the dietary questions. No speech of Paul is recorded at all; there is no mention of Titus.

Whichever version is historical is not the question, though the account by Paul is surely more likely since (1) he was there and (2) he was reporting it relatively soon after its occurrence. The version in Acts could well be a grouping together of several or many meetings on these same subjects, dramatically compacted here, complete with speeches to underscore its importance. The difference is a difference of purpose. Paul is using the event as a historical proof that the whole Church agrees not to force Gentiles to accept Jewish customs. Luke is using the event on a more symbolic level to show that the focus of Christian concern is not on the holy land or the holy city anymore but on the evangelization of the whole world. No preconceived limits should be set to that work. It must be remembered too that Paul wrote before the destruction of Jerusalem in 70 A.D. and Luke wrote after it. And that cataclysmic event more or less removed Palestinian Christianity from the scene as the central community.

The Jews revolted against Rome in 66 A.D., beginning a war they hoped Yahweh would help them win. When the war ended tragically, Palestinian

Christians were caught in the middle: The Romans considered them Jews, the Jews considered them apostates. Many of them fled to other Christian communities around the empire, taking with them their collections of Jesus' sayings and deeds. To an audience outside Palestine—which was used to the more philosophical and theological treatment of the message they had received from the missionaries—the effect of these concrete stories and statements of Jesus must have been tremendous. And this interaction of the more theological material with the more historical-mythic material was certainly responsible in no small part for the writing of the gospels of Luke and Matthew.

Probably during the Jewish War of 66–70 A.D., the version of the Good News according to Mark was already being written, very likely in Rome. Knowing of the attempts of Caligula to erect "the desolating abomination" in the temple and hearing word of the carnage of the war, seeing all around him Christians persecuted by orthodox Jews and martyred by Nero, Mark could not have helped but think that the details of the prophecy of Daniel and the eschatological prophecies of Jesus were on the verge of being literally fulfilled. As we have seen when studying Mark 13, a whole chapter of his gospel was given to Jesus' eschatalogical discourse.

But other concerns were reflected in his gospel as well and, with a brief account of the Passion, scattered anecdotes, sayings, and brief collections of writings, he set out to construct a book which would explain "The Way" of Christian belief. Nearly 20 percent of Mark's gospel (about 117 verses) is taken up with so-called controversy stories which give us a very good idea of the issues that troubled the people in the Christian community for whom Mark was writing.

The treatment Mark gives the passion account which he inherited attempted to answer the very obvious question: *Why* did Jesus die? And why did he die such an apparently shameful death? Why would people desire his death and why would God allow it? To these questions Mark attempts an answer. First of all, Jesus died because the Jewish leaders refused to believe him and, out of envy (15:10), handed him over to Pilate. (The reasons for their envy will come clear in a moment when we consider the controversy stories with which Mark prefaces his treatment of the Passion narrative.) Jesus died because he willed to die: Jesus said, "For the Son of Man himself did not come to be served but to serve, and to give his life as a ransom for many" (10:45). If Jesus did not die and rise, we would never have known that we too would die but arise. But most important, Jesus died because God willed it, and had expressed his will throughout the Hebrew Scriptures: Jesus

said, "Yes, the Son of Man is going to his fate, as the scriptures say he will" (14:21a); and in the Garden, 'Abba (Father)!' he said, 'Everything is possible for you. Take this cup away from me. But let it be as you, not I, would have it.'" And at the crucifixion the details are taken from the Psalms of the Suffering Servant.

In the controversy stories which occupy almost a fifth of his gospel, Mark attempts to answer other questions using the literary device of placing the question in the mouth of Jesus' antagonists, the Scribes and Pharisees, and giving either the answer Jesus himself historically gave or one which was consistent with his message. These can be grouped under disputes which Mark's later audience had (1) with Jews, (2) with the Graeco-Roman environment, or (3) with both. Remember, too, that these answers of Mark were not merely defensive, against attack from Jews and Hellenists, but also offensive—seeking out converts and instructing the already converted. These are some of the questions he attempted to provide answers for in his gospel:

(1) *For Jews:* the Sabbath observance, divorce, the "greatest commandment," the Davidic descent of the Messiah, and food regulations.

(2) *For non-Jews:* the problem of paying tribute to Caesar when that money could be used immorally (exactly the same as the moral problem over paying taxes for the Vietnam war or being civilly disobedient).

(3) *For both:* the source of Jesus' power and the source of his authority, the need for signs to prove beyond doubt Jesus was Lord, defense of eating with pagans and "sinners."

There were also other questions troubling his audience. For instance, who were the true leaders of the Church? Mark's answer is simple: "the Twelve" (3:13–19). What was the relation of John the Baptizer's doctrine and followers to Jesus' doctrine and followers? It is clear to Mark that John was the "Elijah" who was to return to prepare the way of the Lord; he was not Jesus' rival but his herald. Was martyrdom for the sake of others, like Jesus' martyrdom, the only true test of discipleship? Throughout the gospel, Mark's Jesus gives a far less terrifying demand—faith in Jesus as Lord and in the plan of God, humbling oneself, giving a cup of water, living in peace, being wary of riches, childlike vulnerability. In other words, the true test of Christian discipleship is complete renunciation of selfishness for Christ's sake and the sake of the kingdom. Still, for Mark's audiences in and around the Rome of the ferocious Nero, complete renunciation might well mean martyrdom.

But one can imagine the effect of this gospel on the meetings of the frightened, persecuted Christians in Rome and throughout the empire, in danger at any moment of being hung up as living torches in Nero's gardens or thrown to the beasts in the arena. Here is a Jesus, compassionate and willing to help, a friend of sinners; here is a Jesus, hated and despised, betrayed by his friend, deserted by his disciples and sent to shameful death at the hands of Jews and Romans. Surely it was a precious document to them.

But besides the Apocalypse of Chapter 13, the Passion account, and the controversies handed on to him, Mark is quoted by some as having a fourth major source of material for his version of the message: the testimony of Peter himself. Papias of Hieropolis, writing in the early second century, stated:

> *When Mark became Peter's interpreter, he wrote down accurately although not in order, all that he remembered of what the Lord had said or done. For he had not heard or followed the Lord, but later, as I said, (heard and followed) Peter, who used to adapt his teaching to the needs (of the moment), without making any sort of arrangement of the Lord's oracles. Consequently, Mark made no mistake in thus writing down certain things as he remembered them. For he was careful not to omit or falsify anything of what he heard.* The Jerome Biblical Commentary, 42:1

And Mark's gospel was written (65–70) only a few years after Peter's death in Rome (around 64 A.D.). When it was written, the character of Peter had been transfigured by martyrdom, and it is easy to see how readily those threatened by persecution would understand this perfect disciple who believed so fiercely and yet doubted so often, who loved Jesus dearly and yet failed so frequently, who stood breathless at the Transfiguration and snored through the agony in the Garden, who three times denied the Jesus he loved and yet wept bitterly at his weakness and became a missioner of the message of the resurrection.

The Jesus of Mark is the Son of God, equipped with divine knowledge and power. But he is also the one-time Jewish teacher and prophet, with human feelings and limited knowledge and power. Divinity and humanity interpenetrate each other in Jesus in an inseparable unity. He is more than the Messiah; he is the son of God. Mark does not reflect *how* one could be both God and human at the same time, nor how God's son arrived or

departed. But in his rugged Greek prose—so different from the elegance of Luke—he affirmed his belief in a forthright tone that seemed to say, "Don't ask me to explain it, but that's the way things *are*." It is the same tone as Peter's answer to Jesus' question of who they thought Jesus was. "Peter spoke up and said, 'You are the Christ.'" Period. It is the same tone as the tough Gentile centurion's at the cross in the statement that climaxes Mark's gospel: "Truly, this man was the Son of God." Period.

Sections of the New Testament
Approximate Dates of their Composition
(as opposed to their printed order in our Bibles)

Early 50's	1 Thessalonians
	2 Thessalonians
Late 50's	Galatians
	1 Corinthians
	2 Corinthians
	Romans
	Philippians (?)
Early 60's	Philippians (?)
	Philemon
	Colossians
	Ephesians
Mid 60's	MARK
	1 Timothy
	Titus
	2 Timothy
	1 Peter
70's—80's	MATTHEW
	LUKE-ACTS
	Jude
	James
	Hebrews
90's	JOHN
	Apocalypse
	Epistles of John

This chart should not be taken as a hard-and-fast, conclusively historical list—like the dates and succession of American presidents. The writers did not have our modern passion for dating and accuracy. If Paul himself, for instance, is not the author of the letters to Timothy and Titus, they should probably be dated in the 80's. However, most scholars would accept this tentative list, each with his own reservations here and there. (The source is the JBC, 67:57.)

5

THE COMPOSITION OF THE GOSPELS

As I sit here trying to map out this chapter on how the gospel texts emerged, I suddenly realize how like the evangelists' work my own work is. I am not a Scripture scholar in any sense of the word; I am a teacher, trying to take something I really believe in and want to share, something I've studied a good deal on a graduate level, and put it into terms that are both understandable to an upper high school and lower college audience but also in terms that will not simplify-and-falsify.

So I sit here at a desk littered with all kinds of books and notes from other books. They vary in their heaviness, both academic and physical. There is the *Jerusalem Bible*, Perrin's *Introduction*, *The Jerome Biblical Commentary*, Grant's book on the origin and growth of the gospels. I have books that are only about Luke, books that are only about the parables. I even have the Monarch Notes on the New Testament, just in case! But none of them is geared to *my* audience of bright, disinterested students, or even perhaps adults who have left their religious education back in school. Even the texts that are geared for college students seem to require something more like a seminary background in order to be understood.

So I read them all. I borrow a bit here, a bit there, follow this person's outline where it suits my purposes, someone else's when that fits. Mostly I have to piece together what all these people say, to add my own insights and my knowledge of the receptivities of my particular audience, and then write away. For instance, the blending of literary and biblical uses of figurative language at the beginning of this book is something I have never seen anywhere else, but when I checked it with my friends in biblical studies, they said it was not only justified but useful.

, Much the same thing happens with all scholarship. There are a few geniuses, like Einstein or Teilhard de Chardin, whose work is at the outer reaches of human knowledge. Their publications are so technical, so involved, so abstract that they can be communicated only with a few others who, though they themselves do not do original work on that creative level, can still comprehend these new ideas and "translate them downward" to college students, government officials, and readers of more academic magazines. Once again, these students "translate downward" for high school students and Sunday supplements and news magazines. In this way, the ideas gradually percolate down to the ordinary person in the street—in a highly diluted form, but hopefully in an honest form.

The same thing, or something like it, happens with the Scriptures. Jesus, the God-Man, revealed his earthshaking message of resurrection. Then Spirit-filled men like Paul and Peter and the evangelists did their best to "translate downward" to ordinary people this message they understood so well. And what we as individuals receive in our turn is limited only by our intellectual abilities on the one hand and our depth of faith on the other. This is where the analogy to scientific writing breaks down, because the apostles and evangelists were not only trying to pass on ideas, but were also actively engaged in trying to stir up an inner, personal response to it.

Moreover, the evangelists were not helped (or burdened) by our present-day armory of scientific research: accurate statistics, government reports, offical documents, catalogues, surveys, etc. They had the testimony of eye-witnesses and a few scattered scrolls containing an outline of the Passion story and the founding of the Eucharist, plus a few collections of miracle stories, controversy stories, parables, and perhaps a skeleton of an apocalyptic discourse. And, of course, the Hebrew Scripture.

This is what Mark had in front of him when he sat down to write the first gospel: some information, but more importantly a purpose. Mark and the other evangelists did not pretend to have the studied objectivity of a television newscaster when they sat down to report the Good News. They had a

point to make, and each one made that point in his own particular way. And let us not pretend that, no matter how a modern journalist strives for objectivity, none of his or her personal convictions and opinions don't "leak" through in the choice of a particular word rather than another or even in the choice of which stories deserve putting on the air.

The evangelists, too, picked and chose from the materials they had inherited—as I pick and choose what materials in the books I've read would help my students or readers and what would merely confuse them uselessly. All of the evangelists wanted to get across the same basic point: the Good News about the kingdom which had been sown and was growing. But each presented it in his own way, each with an *eye* to *his* particular audience and each inescapably influenced by his own personal insights into the message.

Perhaps this will be clearer if we look at an actual passage from the Passion, where the three synoptic gospels are most alike.

MATTHEW 27	MARK 15	LUKE 23
[51]*And* behold, *the curtain of the temple was torn in two, from top to bottom;* and the earth shook and the rocks were split. [52]The tombs also were opened, and many bodies of the saints who had fallen asleep were raised. [53]And coming out of the tombs after his resurrection they went into the holy city and appeared to many.	[38]*And the curtain of the temple was torn in two from top to bottom.*	[see v. 45]
[54]When *the centurion* and those who were with him, keeping watch over Jesus, *saw* the earthquake and what took place, they were filled with awe, and said, "Truly *this was* the Son of God!"	[39]And when *the centurion,* who stood facing him, *saw* that he thus breathed his last, he said, "Truly *this man was* the Son of God!"	[47]Now when *the centurion saw* what had taken place, he praised God, and said, "Certainly *this man was* innocent!" [48]And all the multitudes who assembled to see the sight, when they saw what had taken place, returned home, beating their breasts.

As an exercise, take a pencil and draw a solid line under words and phrases where the three or even two men agree verbatim (although this is only second-best compared to doing it in the Greek original). Then draw a broken line under words and phrases which are more or less the same, just a difference in vocabulary or style. Finally, circle the places where only one of the three has an entry.

It is obvious that all three have *similarities*. They are all speaking of the same historical event: the death of Jesus. It is also obvious that the three have common details: the centurion and the people and their reactions to Jesus' death. But there are just as obvious *differences*:

1. *Luke* has already put the detail of the curtain being torn in his verse 45, at the moment *before* Jesus died. The event itself is probably only symbolic rather than the recording of an actual historical occurrence. The curtain is the one which hung in front of the Holy of Holies and symbolized the most sacred place in the Jewish cult. But why does Luke put it *before* Jesus' death rather than after as the other two did? Probably to say in symbolic terms that it was Judaism which was defeated at this moment and not Jesus.

2. *Matthew* adds far more of these symbolic apocalyptic details: an earthquake, tombs opening and yielding up their dead, and even more Hebrew saints coming to life again after the resurrection of Jesus. Throughout his gospel, Matthew has a fondness for the apocalyptic form. The earthquake—which Old Testament poetry said figuratively were the footsteps of Yahweh as he passed by—is a sign which says God is leaving Israel behind. Also it is surely one of the signs of the beginning of the Day of Yahweh when the remnant of Israel would be freed. Moreover, through this symbol of the arisen dead, he can connect the resurrection of the believer with the resurrection of Jesus. That is *why* the Messiah had to die. And Matthew was speaking to a Jewish audience who would grasp these allusions far more readily than Gentiles or ourselves.

3. Note carefully the declaration after Jesus' death. *Mark*, writing primarily for Gentiles, has this supreme declaration come from the lips of a Roman. Matthew, writing for Jews, says the testimony came not only from the Roman centurion but from "those who were with him," and the Romans testified in words, but the Jews of Jesus' time would not. Moreover, the holy men of Israel's past testified to Jesus' divinity by their "rising." Luke, writing for an educated Hellenistic audience, has the official Roman witness, the centurion, declare that he was certainly innocent—i.e., not guilty of any crime

against the Roman state. And the "multitudes," the Jews, return to their homes acknowledging their guilt.

Each of the three tells of the same event, but each from a different point of view, for a different audience and with a different purpose. Historically, who knows what the people who actually stood at the cross thought or said? The point is that Jesus actually did die, and that event and its aftermath, the resurrection, called for a response.

The gospels of Matthew, Mark, and Luke are called the "synoptic gospels," from the Greek word *synoptikos,* "seeing the whole thing together." It is the same root as for "synopsis." They tell much the same story in much the same way, and they can be set in parallel columns, as they were above, so that all three can be "seen together." The Gospel of John is the same basic story, too, but told from such a different point of view and with such a mystical, theological tone that we will not deal with it further in these pages except incidentally.

Similarities. The first three gospels have more or less the same content. They report many of the same words and deeds of Jesus, the same miracles, parables, discussions, and events. In some sections, all three will be verbally almost identical; in others, two will be identical. A glance at a book like Throckmorton's *Gospel Parallels,* which lines up the passage from the Passion above, makes this visually apparent.

The plot arrangement of the three gospels is also more or less parallel: The activities of the Baptist are described, Jesus is baptized by him and enters the desert where Satan (the symbol of worldly selfishness) tempts him to throw over his mission and join "everybody else." He then begins his public life, preaching and healing in Galilee, and finally begins his last journey to Jerusalem and to his death and resurrection. The accounts of the Passion are where the three are most nearly identical.

The language is frequently exactly the same, even in places where all three agree on an Old Testament quotation *against* the *Septuagint* translation, the Greek version which Hellenistic Jews accepted. Sometimes all three will use the same unusual Greek syntax or the same comparatively rare Greek words.

Differences. Some speeches and events are recounted by only two of the synoptics; others are used by only one. Sometimes two accounts of the same event will be quite different, at least in emphasis and details chosen. Mark, for instance, has no account of Jesus' birth, while Matthew and Luke do. Even then, the two who do describe Jesus' birth and infancy differ widely.

For example, Matthew has the Magi but no shepherds; Luke has shepherds but no Magi.

Even though the general progression of events is parallel in all three, there are some differences in arrangement of materials too. Where one author groups a clump of material together in one place, another may scatter it throughout his work. Matthew groups his materials into five great discourses, each focusing on a common theme. Luke, however, organized his materials around a single journey to Jerusalem. Even individual sections are organized differently. One need only see the differences in the versions of the Our Father or the Beatitudes to recognize this.

FORM CRITICISM

How did all this happen? One way to approach the question is called form criticism. It is a highly technical, scholarly, scientific study of the linguistic forms of the Greek New Testament. It tries to discern beneath strange Greek sentence structures the original Aramaic in which Jesus or the very earliest community stated the original orally, before it was ever written down. It also studies additions to the original which can be determined, for instance, by customs which came later than the time of Jesus or were proper to other cultures than the Palestinian culture. Further, they study concerns and questions which arise in the text as if they were current at the time of Jesus, whereas such questions and concerns did not actually arise until after his death. From their linguistic studies, form critics isolate various forms Jesus used in teaching: narratives, discourses, sayings, parables, miracle stories, interpretations of Scripture and controversies, etc. By studying the developments of such forms in other non-scriptural Jewish writings and in Hellenistic writings, they can show how not only the form was adapted in later years, but also the content.

Form criticism treats the evangelists as *collectors*, and their science tries to see *how the synoptics' materials came to them.* Within the texts they can pick out the remnants of material which was most likely organized and structured before it came into the evangelist's hands. They can see, for instance, chains of material linked together by a word clue—much like the material of a modern stand-up comic which goes from a joke about one's mother-in-law in a car to a joke about a car in a crash to an airplane crash to a stewardess joke, and on and on. The subject matter of the jokes has nothing in common, but one word from one joke hooks into one word in

the next—because it's easier for the comic to remember them that way. The teachers and preachers in the early Church probably used the same gimmick.

Scholars can also discern clumps of material grouped around a common subject, even though Jesus may have said the individual sentences at different times. They can isolate, too, passages which look as if they may have been drawn up for liturgical purposes in the early community or as handbooks for new converts. This does not mean that the gospels are just made up of bits and pieces, one-liners that Jesus got off at various times and places. He was a teacher, and his audiences, as we said, had far better-developed memories than we have.

Patterns begin to emerge. These scholars discover certain principles at work in the three versions of the one gospel. For instance, wherever the three agree, it is the order of Mark which is followed. Matthew's and Mark's versions may agree against Luke's, but Matthew and Luke never agree *against* Mark. That sounds as complicated as a math formula, but it really is not. In the passage we saw above from the Passion, Mark and Matthew have the curtain torn after Jesus' death; Luke has it before. Mark and Luke omit the apocalyptic symbols of the earthquake and the opening tombs; Matthew includes them. Mark and Matthew have the centurion saying "Son of God"; Luke has him saying "innocent."

The point is that Luke and Matthew never agree *against* Mark. They may have material Mark does not have at all, where the texts in Luke and Matthew will be almost identical (the Q source). But there is no place where all three treat the same passage in which Mark has one version and Matthew and Luke agree on a different version. This consistent pattern of agreement not only in the general overall order of events but in actual verbal agreement shows that the gospel of Mark was written first and that Matthew and Luke had a copy of Mark on their desks as they wrote.

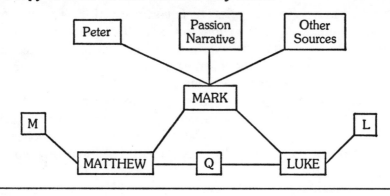

Therefore, some sections of the synoptic gospels are common to all three. These sections were originally in Mark and were included almost unedited in Matthew's and Luke's new edition of Mark. In a large part, Matthew and Luke have edited, revised, abridged, and amplified Mark.

Furthermore, there are sections of Matthew and Luke which are so close verbally that they must be using another common source (Q), which was apparently not available to Mark (since he does not include such good material).

Still further, there are sections both in Matthew and in Luke which are unique to each of them, which shows that each of them had his own special collections of material (L for Luke's source and M for Matthew's) which was unavailable to the other.

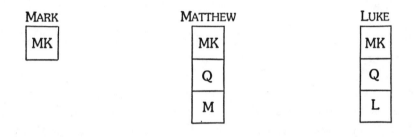

Finally, we cannot omit the fact (as we will see with redaction criticism) that each of the three synoptics felt free to alter even his common material, interpret it differently, and fabricate further symbolic statements (e.g., Matthew's earthquake) which furthered his personal overall purpose in writing his version of the message.

As a result of their researches, then, form critics believe they can isolate more than a few stages in the composition of "the gospel before the gospels," clumps of material which had been formulated in various communities during the thirty years between the Resurrection and the time the gospels were beginning to be written. What follows is by no means as simplified or clear-cut as it appears on this page, but it will serve at least as an introduction.

In the diagram above, the three snoptic gospels are indicated by boxes. But, as the lines indicate, these final editions resulted from transmission first by oral communication, then through various written collections to the evangelist. The earliest sources are clear. The circled letters are:

Q = The sayings source we have already seen, about 250 verses common to Luke and Matthew but not found in Mark.

M= Material found in Matthew alone, coming for a source or sources unknown to either Mark or Luke.

L= Material found in Luke alone, coming from a source or sources unknown to either Mark or Matthew.

Therefore,

Mark= Peter's recollections + a Passion outline + other sources + Old Testament.

Matthew = Mark + the Q collection + M, a source or sources unknown to Mark or Luke (e.g., Magi at the Nativity).

Luke= Mark + the Q collection + L, a source or sources unknown to Mark or Matthew (e.g., shepherds at the Nativity).

But form criticism is not enough. The evangelists were not mere robots or computers assembling data. They were themselves Spirit-filled men, just as Paul and Peter had been. There is behind their separate works a recognizable person whose individual concerns and emphases are apparent throughout the individual book and unify it as the product of one man's single vision of the common data, no matter where they had been or in what form they had been before they came to him.

REDACTION CRITICISM

Redaction criticism treats the evangelists as *authors*, and their science tries to see *what the synoptics did to the material* handed down to them. In studying dominant themes proper to each evangelist, differing plot structure, different use of the same characters, and especially what they add which the others don't have, critics see three very different human beings at work on the same basic message and even on the same basic sources. In knowing each of the three as a personality, the ordinary reader can get far more richness out of knowing how each version was written from a particular and personal viewpoint.

Mark: The Roman Realist

It is too bad that all of our translations of the gospels are done either all by one person or by some kind of committee, rather than by individuals who could bring out the flavor of each evangelist's Greek. Mark is the briefest of

the gospels, with a severe outline and a rugged style, spare and without embellishments. For example, when Jesus commands the winds and the waves to be silent, he does not use the "Peace! Be still!" of our cautious translations. The Greek is really more like our "Shut up!" Mark has a job to do, and he does not have the same amount of time for Matthew's extensive theologizing or Luke's elegant style.

Mark is stern, facing the desperate issues confronting the faithful in a persecuted Church, a people perhaps even facing martyrdom. He must persuade his audience to hang on, despite the inducements of the pagans to give in and live a materialist life—or face the lions.

He is less sympathetic to Judaism than Matthew or Luke; in fact he does not betray much knowledge of Judaism. That is not the principal problem facing him and his audience. Instead, he builds his gospel as the revelation of the messianic secret. It is amazing to see how frequently he describes Jesus' cures as cures of blindness, external physical blindness as a symbol of internal self-blindedness. And the messianic secret is gradually revealed in three climactic moments: Peter's recognition of Jesus as the Messiah (8:27), Jesus' reply at his trial that he is indeed "the Son of the Blessed One," and finally the climactic, forthright opening of the centurion's eyes: "Truly, this was the Son of God!"

Matthew: The Jewish Theologian-Teacher

Matthew himself—and Matthew alone—writes the parable of the householder: "Every scribe who has been trained for the kingdom of God is like a householder who brings out of his treasure what is new and what is old" (13:52). He could be describing himself, offering his readers the treasures of both the Old and the New Covenants. Indeed, he could have been a scribe or a rabbi himself, steeped in the Hebrew Scriptures and its law. His gospel is filled with Old Testament quotations and allusions, in an attempt to prove— doubtless to a Jewish audience—that the promise of the law and the prophets has been fulfilled, that Jesus *is* the Messiah, and that the Christian community is the remnant of the New Israel.

After the disastrous fall of Jerusalem in 70 A.D., the orthodox Jew saw the land of his fathers lying in heaps. His temple and its Sadducean priesthood had disappeared. For him, it was almost literally the end of the world as he knew it. The only thing left was to strengthen what remained, and so many of the Scribes and Pharisees retired to the town of Jamnia and began to study and reorganize the law and its interpretations. Henceforth, Judaism

could not be focused on the temple, but it would carry on as a religion centered in the school and the synagogue. Thus it has remained since that time until our own day.

Matthew attempted the same kind of study of the gospel message as the Scribes were doing of the law. Reflecting on the message of the kingdom and on the data handed down to him from the earliest days, he wrote what was equivalently a Christian supplement to the Hebrew Scriptures. In five discourses, which paralleled the five books of the Hebrew Pentateuch, he set out to develop his astonishing insight that Jesus is the new Moses, but an even greater teacher than Moses. Jesus is the Messiah of Old Testament hopes—not a warrior or prophet or priest in the literal way that they expected, but all those things summed up and transfigured by his role as the long-prophesied suffering servant of Yahweh.

Despite his rabbinic methods, Matthew is the most violently anti-Pharisaic of all the evangelists. Reading the woes that Jesus calls down on the Pharisees in Matthew's twenty-third chapter is enough to make one shudder. And these woes will fall on them because they rejected the Messiah. And, unlike them, Matthew still nourishes an apocalyptic hope that Yahweh would indeed transform the world, but through people on fire with the Spirit of Jesus.

Matthew's interests are Jewish: the law, the messianic hope, the fulfillment of prophecy, the duties of worship, prayer, fasting, and almsgiving. Although he agrees with Paul about the worldwide dimension of the message outside Judaism, he has no sympathy with the seemingly wide-open interpretation Paul had of the freedom of the sons of God. With typical teacher's organization, he gathers his material before the Passion into five great discourses of Jesus: (1) on discipleship (The Sermon on the Mount); (2) on apostleship and spreading the word, once it's learned; (3) on the hidden revelation (The Parables of the Kingdom); (4) on church administration; (5) on the fulfillment of the kingdom in the day of Yahweh. And then the Passion, the beginning of the kingdom.

Luke: The Hellenistic Storyteller

Luke-Acts—which were undoubtedly written by the same writer—takes up about one-quarter of the whole New Testament. It is a sweeping study of the historic message, first of Jesus, ending in Jerusalem, then of Peter and Paul and the early community, ending in Rome, the center of the known

world. And it is told by a poet-historian of elegant style and wonderfully sensitive humanity.

Only in Luke do we get the table talk, the friendliness, the great parables of human kindness and goodness (like The Good Samaritan and The Prodigal Son). Only in Luke are the harshness and loathesomeness of Jesus' treatment during the Passion toned down; one might almost suspect that Luke cannot tolerate thinking that such a person could be so treated. The author of Luke's version has an observant eye for mannerisms, reactions, hidden motivations. And he has a broadminded openness to all groups and peoples: swineherds, Samaritans, lepers, publicans, soldiers, shepherds, prostitutes, the poor. It is interesting to check a list like Throckmorton's, which parallels the three gospels, and see the stories and parables which Luke has which the other two synotpics do not: the shepherds at Bethlehem, the widow at Nain, the Good Samaritan, Martha and Mary, the blessedness of Jesus' mother, the Prodigal Son, the Rich Man and Lazarus, healing the ten lepers, little Zaccheus in his sycamore tree, the disciples' pitiful armory of only two swords, the disciples on the road to Emmaus, and the Ascension of Jesus. Luke's is a gospel of mercy.

Luke has a sympathy for Judaism, but his introduction to Theophilus which opens his gospel hints that he aims to attract and interest cultured readers—both to find converts and to ward off suppression by the Romans. He takes great pains to show his specific audience that there was nothing politically subversive or revolutionary about Jesus or his followers: after all, they had only two swords! Only Luke has the Roman procurator, Pilate, declare officially and explicitly, "I find no crime in this man." In Mark, Pilate orders Jesus' death "to satisfy the [Jewish] crowd"; in Matthew it is "out of fear of a riot" but in Luke it is "to answer the demand of the Jews."

These are three different men, bringing their own special talents, interests, and insights to the materials handed down to them—some of which they all had available to them (at least through Mark), some of which Matthew and Luke shared, some of which Matthew and Luke had independently of one another. But their special interests did not blind them to the needs beyond their particular audiences. After all, it was only Matthew, the Jew, who included the Gentile Magi, and it was only Luke, the Hellenist, who included the Jewish shepherds—as the official witnesses to the birth of Jesus. And the aim of all three was fundamentally the same: to present the same multifaceted Lord and his message of liberation from death.

PART TWO

Bringing the Word Alive Again: the Synoptic Passions

6

THE ARREST OF JESUS

WHY BEGIN AT THE END?

The Gospel of Luke is 24 chapters long: the first 21 chapters cover 30 years of Jesus' life; the last 3 chapters cover 2½ days. For this reason someone has rightly said that each gospel is "a Passion narrative preceded by a biography." That's right. And there's a reason.

As we have said, the Passion is the most primitive gospel narrative. There were sayings of Jesus which circulated like the Beatitudes and the Our Father and the words of consecration at the Last Supper, sayings which had been memorized and even gathered into written collections. But the people in the early Church were above all "witnesses to the resurrection" (Acts 1:22, 2:32, 3:15, etc., I Cor 15:14, Rom 10:9). That is the Good News; that's what they celebrated at their weekly Eucharists. For a while, then, that Good News was enough.

But one does have to ask questions. If Jesus rose from the dead, it follows as the night the day that he had to die first, right? How did he die? Why did he die? "I thought you said he was God!" And so, very brief oral collections were drawn up gathering together the details of the most crucial and focal moments leading up to the event: the Resurrection. (Just as the event in the history of Israel, the exodus, was more important than what

preceded it, still a deeper understanding of that monumental moment is helped by knowing the events that built up to it.)

The Passion stories were the first formal narratives composed about the life of Jesus—the first attempt at more than random recollections of things Jesus did, a story that progresses as all stories do, from place to place and time to time. It had a *beginning* which showed the characters and the tensions between them; an *incentive moment,* some event that thrust into the tensions and triggered the action of the story; a gradually building *series of scenes* showing the interplay between the protagonist and his antagonists; a *climax* where the hero could still escape; a *last confrontation* in which the "bad guys" seemed to win; and a *happy ending* where the protagonist abruptly foils his antagonists.

How does the shrewd reporter or detective know that the Passion was the first narrative developed about the life of Jesus—and not some other section of his life, like the Infancy narratives or the journey toward Jerusalem? We have no certainty; nobody sat down and wrote out how the gospels were gradually gathered together. But there are some heavy clues.

First, we know how important stories tend to be filled out. When the Watergate news first broke, it was just a brief news story about some men caught in the Democratic National Headquarters. But over the course of two years, look at the volumes upon volumes of data that grew out of it! It was like pulling on a single thread and dragging out acres of unsuspected yarns.

But the more reporters unearth solid data and the more writers organize and interpret them, the more versions you get. Some reporters pull this particular bit of data first; some hold it for a snappy climax to an article. You find this same practice throughout the gospels. There are certain basic chronological facts that are unchangeable: Jesus began with his baptism by John in the Jordan, went around preaching, and ended on a cross in Jerusalem. Those are the skeletal facts and all good reporters and evangelists have to adhere to them.

But since there were no diaries or logs of Jesus' activities as there were in Watergate (simply because the people of the day weren't as conditioned to fanatic clock-watching as we are), it didn't make that much difference when Jesus said such and such or did such and such; the fact he did it and the probing for what it meant were far more important. Therefore, you'll find Luke has Jesus picking all twelve apostles and then giving the Beatitudes sermon at the base of a hill; Matthew, on the other hand, has Jesus picking four fishermen, giving substantially the same but an expanded Beatitudes

sermon on top of a hill, and then choosing the other apostles later. What difference when or where, as long as he chose them? And the Beatitudes are as true whether they were first spoken on the top of a hill or at the bottom of another hill entirely. Both Matthew and Luke had their own sources of information on exact times and places—sometimes conflicting. But more important, since the events themselves were more significant than pinpointing the time and place of their occurrence, the first writers were primarily interested in discovering what meaning the deeds and sayings of Jesus could have for the Christian and the interested pagan. Therefore, both Matthew and Luke arranged those events (which could have happened in a different actual sequence) into a sequence which more fully enriched the total appreciation of that same Christian message each shared with the other, in his own way.

Just as two jewelers will design different settings for the same precious gem, Matthew and Luke (and Mark and John) designed different settings. But it was the same jewel.

Strangely, though, unlike the organization of the episodes in Jesus' public life, the Passion sections of all four gospels are not very different at all from one another. If you look at the gospels of Mark and John before the Passion, the outlines are very different. But when you come to the entry into Jerusalem, all four gospels begin to become far more similar in their order of progression. These events—or this one event as a developing wholeness—was far too sacred to juggle around with too much. As a result, Mark still differs from John, and somewhat even from Matthew and Luke, up until the arrest in the Garden. From then on—with little personal adjustments here and there—they are singing precisely the same song in the same rhythm—moving through the same places at the same times with the same sayings. Even John's style, which is the most distinctive throughout, changes at the moment of the arrest. All four writers are handling material which has already become sacred and established in the memories of their listeners. The basic account—beginning with the arrest—had been formulated very early in the primitive Church: solemn, schematic, and written in rather good Greek. Each of the four writers fiddled a bit here and there, but they wouldn't tamper with substantials.

Since the gospels' structures are most similar to one another in the Passion accounts (from the arrest onward), the slight differences may more easily betray the particular interests and intentions of each author. So we begin with the Passion accounts.

A further reason why the Passion accounts would very likely be the first narratives written by the early Church is that they deal with a problem the early Church must have faced—a problem also far more important than absolute stop-watch accuracy. In dealing with converts and with Christians of flagging faith, the early Church had to cope with the scandal of the cross— the apparent failure of Christ (and therefore of God) on Calvary.

Even during his lifetime, Jesus faced angered disbelief—even from Peter, his most typical disciple—when he predicted the degradation that he saw was inevitable for him. But Peter's reaction both to the predictions and to the actuality of the Passion were the normal human reaction: "No! He's too good, too special! It's hard enough to accept a God who can let a good person suffer sickness and death, but not him! And surely not walking into it with his eyes wide open. He's the best of us! No God could be good and allow that, much less seem to demand it."

In the light of this inevitable reaction, it's surprising at first that the evangelists didn't play down the darkness and the horror of the Passion. (Luke softens it a touch here and there, but he will not avoid the unavoidable truth: It was ugly.) And yet the forthright way in which the writers handle the bruising contradictions of the God-man's last hours shows that from the beginning Christianity was not a religion either of unrelieved light or of evasion. The Passion, they realized, was not a brief and unfortunate little interlude that could be smiled over in a few well-chosen phrases. Nor on the other hand was it a defeat. It was an ugly combat—but an ultimately victorious combat. The cross is the crux of Christianity.

For this reason the evangelists stress two things: first, Jesus' foreknowledge of the unavoidable climax and his free consent to it; and second, the constant recurrence of quotations from the Old Testament which show that from the beginning, this particular fate was God's will for Christ himself. And remember that to the ears of a Jewish audience which from childhood had been steeped in the Old Testament, even a single word, even a similar rhythm of phrase brought echoes of the prophecies of the Passion. For the Gentiles of Luke's audience—including ourselves—who are not that familar with the Old Testament, he and the other evangelists make explicit Old Testament references again and again. Granted these are only hints of the entire Hebrew passage referred to, but if you take the time to trace them from the footnotes in your text to the full Old Testament source, you will get some beginning of an idea how this interweaving of the two testaments enrich one another and give the reader—then and now—a firm conviction of the purposeful evolution of man's destiny in the patient hands of God.

THE GOSPEL ACCOUNTS

What you are about to read is not a biographical account of the last hours of a dead hero. You are about to study the testament of three men's faith in the risen Lord and in the Father who used his son to destroy death.

One preliminary note: Although the evangelists are more fully parallel in the Passion accounts than they are anywhere else in their gospels, this does not claim they are four verbally identical accounts. Despite their strong congruence, each one retains his particular perspective on the same story, his particular style, his particular "axe."

Mark gives the *kerygma*—the irreducible message of the early Church. It is obvious from his helter-skelter style that he's rattling off the story orally, improvising, and that he is so filled with the excitement and the challenge of the thing that he doesn't care that his grammar's not too great, that he doubles back, that he scatter-shoots. He writes like an enthused high school freshman! Not only is he not afraid to stun his audience; he wants to. The cross is a scandal, but God wanted it that way!

Matthew speaks as the voice of the Christian people vs. the voice of the Israelite people. He is careful, clarifying Mark, orderly. He wants his audience to understand this happening and its place in God's slow working of mankind toward fulfillment.

Luke is more cautious even than Matthew. He wants to write with greater attention to style, to narrative "build," to meaningful juxtaposition. He is a Gentile with a sense of the structures and unities of Greek drama. But more than anything he wants to show how the first Christian reacted to defeat with the confidence of a victor—knowing, as Luke did, that many men and women among his audience would face just such accusers, just such judges, just such deaths, and, he trusted, just such resurrections. He is letting the reader "in" to the gospel, as the audience is let "in" to a play, to walk with Jesus. In a sense, he is writing a manual for martyrs.

Thus, there are three things to look for: the absolutely common elements to all three versions, the slightly different outlines, the clearly different emphases. Then we can ask, with such similarities, why does each stress what he does?

When reading the gospels in parallel, it is best to begin with Mark whose text the other two had before them as they wrote. Read the whole Mark text for each section and find where the logical divisions and transitions of each section occur; it's like dividing the scenes of a play into "sub-scenes," signaled by the entrance of a new character or a change of subject. In the

pages which follow, these divisions will be made for you, but after a little practice it should not be difficult to do it for youself. Draw a line across the three columns at each of these structural breaks, and concentrate your attention only on that small, manageable section before going on to the next.

In each of these smaller segments—no more than four or five verses—underline first the exact correspondences with a solid line, then the approximate correspondences with a broken line, and finally circle the material unique to each. Read Mark first, then compare Matthew to Mark, then compare Luke to the two of them. Knowing what each evangelist's interests and audience were, try to see why Mark pictured this situation as he did and then why Matthew and Luke varied his text. If tag-phrases help to keep the three separate, think of Mark, the persecuted Roman realist; Matthew, the Jewish theologian-teacher; Luke, the Hellenistic storyteller who was defending the Christian community from suppression as "perpetrators of shameful deeds."

Jesus Taken Captive

MATTHEW 26	MARK 14	LUKE 22
[47]While he was still speaking, Judas came, one of the twelve, and with him a great crowd with swords and clubs, from the chief priests and the elders of the people.	[43]And immediately, while he was speaking, Judas came, one of the twelve, and with him a crowd with swords and clubs, from the chief priests and the scribes and the elders.	[47]While he was still speaking, there came a crowd, and the man called Judas, one of the twelve, was leading them. [cf. v. 52 below.]
[48]Now the betrayer had given them a sign, saying, "The one I shall kiss is the man; seize him."	[44]Now the betrayer had given them a sign, saying, "The one I shall kiss is the man; seize him and lead him away safely."	
[49]And he came up to Jesus at once and said, "Hail Master!" And he kissed him. [50]Jesus said to him, "Friend, why are you here?" Then they came up and laid hands on Jesus and seized him.	[45]And when he came, he went up to him at once, and said, "Master!" And he kissed him.	

⁴⁶And they laid hands on him and seized him.	He drew near to Jesus to kiss him; ⁴⁸but Jesus said to him, "Judas, would you betray the Son of man with a kiss?"

1. First of all, when you are reading Mark this closely, you may be able to pick up the slightly out-of-kilter style, even in the English translation. Unlike the other two, his style is urgent, breathless, almost as if he were dictating it in a rage at what Judas was doing. "And immediately—while he was still speaking!" Notice too the awkward, "And when he came, he went up." In the Greek it is literally translated: "And coming, immediately coming up to him." Compare it to the same phrases in Matthew who smoothes out the rugged, breathy style.

Finally, note that even though the action of "laying hands on Jesus" and "seizing" him are exactly the same, even Matthew keeps them separate as Mark had them. Why? Perhaps because the thought of such people touching Jesus was equally as repulsive as the thought of his being arrested.

2. Notice how similar Matthew is to Mark. His only changes are to specify that it was a "great" crowd and to use the name "Jesus" to clear up the ambiguity of "him" and "he." Also he cleans up the messy style.

But Matthew does have a few significant additions and deletions. Notice what group Matthew omits from the mob: the scribes. Why? He also omits Mark's puzzling "lead him away safely."

And he adds a remark of Jesus, "Friend, why are you here?" The reason is obvious: It heightens the enormity of what Judas is doing, leading enemies not to his own enemy or to a villain but to a man who still has the large-heartedness to call him "Friend."

Although most versions translate this "why are you here" or "why have you come," in Greek there is no verb in the sentence. Therefore, most commentators would prefer to remain with the less grammatical but more powerful half-sentence: "For what you have come!" or as we might say, "Friend, get on with it!"

3. Luke says that Judas was leading the crowd, not as its appointed head but as a bloodhound seeking out the prey, and he saves the identification of the members of the crowd until later, v. 52. It is a good plot device to keep the listener in suspense.

But the most significant omissions are the use of the kiss as a prear-

ranged signal and the actual kiss itself. Perhaps Luke felt that, Jesus being as well-known as he was, the kiss was not necessary. Some have said that, since the Garden was dark and since the officials didn't want to arrest the whole group of disciples, Judas had used it as a signal. But Luke uses the kiss as the ordinary action by which two Jewish friends of the time would greet one another. The most focal omission is that he drops the words, "And he kissed him." One gets the impression that Jesus prevented it, and perhaps Luke's customary "protectiveness" for Jesus refused to picture such a concretely revolting incident.

Like Matthew, Luke adds a reply of Jesus to Judas's attempt. But the significant difference is that in Luke's version Jesus knows only too clearly why Judas is there. What's more, he puts that action into a context far greater than an incident in a garden or even the betrayal of a friend. This is an action, for Luke, on a cosmic level. This is not just the arrest of a holy rabbi or even of a prophet. This is the betrayal of the Son of Man, whom the prophet Daniel saw coming on the clouds of heaven to take possession of his inheritance, the kingdom.

The Attack on the Slave

MATTHEW 26	MARK 14	LUKE 22
[51]And behold one of those who were with Jesus stretched out his hand and drew his sword and struck the slave of the high priest, and cut off his ear. [52]Then Jesus said to him, "Put your sword back into its place; for all who take the sword will perish by the sword. [53]Do you think that I cannot appeal to my Father, and he will at once send me twelve legions of angels?[54] But how then should the scriptures be fulfilled, that it must be so?"	[47]But one of those who stood by drew his sword, and struck the slave of the high priest and cut off his ear.	[49]And when those who were about him saw what would follow, they said, "Lord, shall we strike with the sword?" [50]And one of them struck the slave of the high priest and cut off his right ear. [51]But Jesus said, "No more of this!" And he touched his ear and healed him.

1. Mark is typically terse. Somebody pulled a sword and cut off the ear of the high priest's slave. That's that. No apologies, no criticism, either from Jesus or from Mark.

2. Matthew specifies that the assailant was actually one of Jesus' followers. Then he alone uses the incident for a statement from Jesus on violence as a solution to problems. But notice that Jesus does not object to violence as being immoral but as being utterly futile.

Furthermore, and more to Matthew's point, he says that armed resistance—whether in Jesus' time or in Matthew's time—will prevent God's will (as expressed in the Scriptures) from being fulfilled.

Finally, it is obvious that Jesus could have escaped this crowd, as he had done before, or even called heavenly power (the symbol of angels) to save him. But he would not. He chooses here to accept the will of the Father, as ordained in the Scriptures and as executed here by the agents of the skeptical hierarchy.

3. Luke shows the disciples asking Jesus if they should fight. In a verse previous to this episode, at the Last Supper (22:38), they have told Jesus about their entire armory: two swords. But someone of their number—only John says that it was Peter and that the slave's name was Malchus—draws a sword and attacks the slave. Only Luke says it was his right ear, and Matthew and Mark use the Greek word for earlobe. It was not a huge battle!

Then Luke pictures Jesus saying, "No more of this!" Equivalently, Jesus is saying, "Hands off! You don't know what you're doing." This is roughly similar to Matthew's statement about using the sword, at that moment or in the future.

Then, in direct contrast to the use of violence, Jesus takes compassion on the hurt man and heals him. This is typically the Luke who himself had such compassion for the outcast. Earlier in their gospels, Matthew and Mark show Jesus performing miracles to show his power and the power of his kingdom over "Satan" and his kingdom. Typically, Luke shows Jesus performing this miracle solely out of human kindness for the wounded man. It is Luke, after all, who is the only evangelist who tells the story of the Good Samaritan.

[55]At that hour Jesus said to the crowds	[48]And Jesus said to them,	[52]Then Jesus said to the chief priests and captains of the temple and elders, who had come out against him, "Have you
"Have you come out as against a robber, with	"Have you come out as against a robber, with	

swords and clubs to capture me?"	swords and clubs to capture me?"	come out as against a robber, with swords and clubs?"

Note the verbal identity in all three of the last sentences. It suggests that this saying was part of the memorized words of Jesus. Although Matthew at times feels free to alter and amplify the very words of Jesus himself, Luke very rarely tampers with the words of Jesus which he finds in Mark.

Day after day I sat in the temple teaching, and you did not seize me.	[49]Day after day I was with you in the temple teaching and you did not seize me.	[53]When I was with you day after day in the temple, you did not lay hands on me. But this is your hour and the power of darkness.
[56]But all this has taken place that the scriptures of the prophets might be fulfilled." Then all the disciples forsook him and fled.	But let the scriptures be fulfilled." And they all forsook him and fled.	
	[51]And a young man followed him, with nothing but a linen cloth about his body; and they seized him. [52]but he left the linen cloth and ran away naked.	

1. The only addition Mark has is the puzzling little picture he tacks onto the end of the episode: a young man fleeing naked. Since Mark is so all-fired in a hurry and here adds something no other gospel has, one must suspect a purpose.

Perhaps one possibility emerges if you will allow a little Greek. The English verb "followed" does not really bring out the full meaning of the Greek verb Mark uses: *sunēkoluthei*, which is really stronger, something like "shadowed" or "followed intimately." Who then is this young man (Greek, *neaniskos*) who is "shadowing" Jesus?

The Greek word *sindon*, a fine unused linen cloth, which is used here, and the Greek adjective *peribeblēmenos*, "thrown about him," and the noun *neaniskos*, "young man," occur again later in Mark's gospel:

In Mark 15:46, Joseph of Arimathea buys a fine linen cloth (*sindōn*) and wraps the body of Jesus in it.

Then when Mark treats the events of Easter morning, the women are greeted not by an angel (as in Matthew) or by two men (as in Luke) but by a "young man," *neaniskon*, with a white cloth "wrapped around him," *peribeblēmenon*. The word for white cloth is not *sindōn*, but it is a white cloth nonetheless.

The verbal similarities between this episode of the Marcan "streaker" and episodes after Jesus' death seem too close for coincidence. They must have some historical basis or else some symbolic significance. But why would Mark, so thrifty with words, include the escape of just one more of the disciples? Perhaps this "young man" is a mythic way of saying some greater truth. Perhaps this is merely another way of describing the ultimate desertion: the loss of the symbolic presence of the Father's protecting power. Angels and young men are frequently used throughout the Old Testament for symbols of God's messages and God's presence. If this young man in white who flees Jesus is a symbol of God's protective presence fleeing Jesus, then he is alone indeed. First his disciples desert him. Then the power of God's felt presence deserts him, too—to return only at the resurrection.

CONJECTURE

2. Matthew and Mark both stress that Jesus freely surrendered himself. They need not have sought him out in such a lonely place. The Passion narratives stress that the Jewish leaders did not want a public arrest, since they couldn't gauge the reaction of the populace—who had greeted Jesus with palms only a week before!

The disciples had offered to use force, but when Jesus rejected that, they didn't know what to do. So they ran.

3. Luke's reason for the power of the crowd over Jesus is more cryptic than merely saying that it was "to fulfill the scriptures." He has Jesus say, "This is your hour, and (this is) the power of darkness." The first half of the statement is merely a concession of this round to the temple, but the second part shows that they themselves are pawns in the hands of a far greater force, the kingdom of Satan, the power of darkness.

Remember that throughout the New Testament the battle is on a cosmic scale. "Satan" is the symbol of all that is selfish and self-destructive in human beings. And surely the Passion is a monument to man's self-destructiveness—the slaughter of the herald of the Good News of immortality.

In the earlier episode where Jesus is tempted by "Satan" in the desert, only in Luke does the tempter offer him *exousia*, "power, authority," if

Jesus will fall down and adore him (i.e., selfishness). That is the same word Luke uses here: "the *exousia* of darkness." And at the end of the temptation scene in the desert, Luke alone says that Satan left him "to return at the appointed time." Here, in the garden, "This is the power of darkness" returning. This is the appointed time.

From the moment of the desert temptation to this moment of arrest, Jesus had gone about his business free of any kind of attack, as if there were a shield around him. Devils infesting possessed people cried out in torment at his approach. But during the Last Supper, the shields begin breaking down. Only in Luke (22:3) does an evangelist say, "Then Satan entered into Judas, called Iscariot." Only in Luke (22:31) does an evangelist connect Peter's denials with the enemy's increasing power, readying for the kill: "Simon, Simon, behold. Satan demanded to have you, that he might sift you like wheat, but I have prayed for you in that your faith may not fail; and when you have turned again, strengthen your brethren."

There is a far stronger climax to Luke's version of this scene than the English translation delivers: "This is the power of darkness." This is in fact the critical moment, the crisis point. After the agony in the garden, Luke's hero has made up his mind; he is ready. The shields are down and Jesus stands utterly alone and naked to his enemy.

This is not merely a struggle between an untamable rabbi and a handful of envious priests. This is a cosmic battle between the darkness and the light.

SUMMARY OF DIFFERENT EMPHASES

Mark

Mark writes with simplicity and a kind of pell-mell breathlessness. He gives very little information; just the bare story, as if he's saying, "Let's get to the climax!" In his account, Jesus says nothing to Judas and nothing to whoever cut off the slave's earlobe. But in his only solo addition Mark puts this episode into a cosmic scale just as solidly as the other two. He clearly associates this moment with the entire Old Testament myth of the way God deals with mankind. At this moment, the Son of Man stands deserted by his followers and by his own conviction of God's protective presence. It is just Jesus and the enemy.

Matthew

Stylistically, Matthew smoothes out Mark's rough Greek style. But his version of the scene shows Jesus as being more than the silent sufferer of Mark's version. He speaks both to Judas and to the swordsman, and uses the incident to make a point about the uselessness of violence, both in the time of Jesus and in the time of Matthew. He explicitly shows that violence will frustrate the plan which God has been revealing to Israel for ages. Because it is the will of the Father that the Hero-Messiah suffer, Jesus freely chooses to accept that will and that suffering.

Luke

Luke's is a more natural narrative style. He shows first the crowd and only then its leader, whom one would pick out only after the initial shock of the group's intrusion. He saves disclosure of the identities of the people in the mob until he has built up the scene, and he alone of the three says they are the temple priests rather than agents sent from the temple priests. Jesus is taken into custody only after the scene, not during it.

Luke is more delicate in his sensibilities and more protective of the person of Jesus, even in his reporting. There is no explicit reference in Luke to the fact that the disciples deserted Jesus, no actual kiss from Judas, but there is instead Jesus' kindly act of healing the wounded man.

Still there is the stern rebuke against using force and, as each of the evangelists does in his own way, Luke also places this event on a cosmic level by his declaration that this is the critical moment, when the power of darkness has unlimited access to Jesus.

SUMMARY OF SIMILARITIES

(1) All three have almost exactly the same skeletal outline or structure:
  a. The crowd and Judas
  b. The kiss
  c. Cutting off the ear
  d. Jesus addressing the crowd regarding their justification for the arrest
  e. The cosmic dimension of the event
  f. Jesus is taken away

(2) In all, the vagueness of the word "crowd" seems to indicate that no

one was precisely sure who the particular individuals were or how large the group was.

(3) The kiss of Judas which all three mention might possibly recall to the well-trained Jewish ear the words of Psalm 55 (13–14, 20–21):

Were it an enemy who insulted me,
    I could put up with that;
had a rival got the better of me,
    I could hide from him.

But you, a man of my own rank,
    a colleague and a friend,
to whom sweet conversation bound me
    in the house of God! . . .

He has attacked his friends,
    he has gone back on his word;
though his mouth is smoother than butter,
    he has war in his heart;
his words may soothe more than oil,
    but they are naked swords.

Or, even more likely, Proverbs 27: "From one who loves, wounds are well-intentioned; from one who hates, kisses are ominous."

(4) When Jesus refuses them the only solution they know—fighting back—the disciples don't know what to do. This passive resistance makes no sense. So they desert him, although Luke discreetly leaves the reader to infer that from what follows. In all three versions, it is fortunate Jesus didn't count on his followers for force, since the best they can do is an ear!

(5) All three have identical words in "Have you come out against a robber, with swords and clubs?"

(6) All three show Jesus asking why the officials did not capture him in some public place and, without waiting for a response, giving the answer himself. Although each does it in his own way, the answer given is one which raises this event far above the simple arrest of an innocent victim. This is a moment in a cosmic battle: In Mark and Matthew, this is the moment when all the Hebrew Scriptures begin to focus; in Mark, it is the moment when Jesus' certitude about God's protecting presence deserts him; in Luke it is the moment when the battle between Jesus and the arch-enemy is joined. And, in all three, Christ freely gives himself up to these self-important little men who, unknowingly, are merely the pawns of Jesus' real enemy.

7

THE SANHEDRIN TRIAL

Before going on to the separate sections of the Sanhedrin trial in each of the three versions, we should have a quick idea of the outline of each in order to avoid confusion. Luke purposefully rearranges the outline of Mark (which Matthew follows), and part of the purpose of this chapter is to determine why. However, despite different placement of events in the two outlines, the development of each segment within each section is more or less parallel in the three accounts.

Outline

MATTHEW AND MARK
A. Introduction: Jesus taken to the high priest's; Peter sitting by the fire.
B. Night trial
C. Mockery and beating
D. Peter's denials and repentance

LUKE
A. Introduction: Jesus taken to the high priest's; Peter sitting by the fire.
D. Peter's denials and repentance
C. Mockery and beating
B. Morning trial

One of the reasons for Luke's placement of the trial in the morning was that night trials were illegal according to Jewish law, and such scrupulous

adherents to the law as these elders would certainly have avoided that. Perhaps Mark and Matthew place it at night to underline the perversion of justice in condemning Jesus—even though Luke's placement is probably more historical. But the injustice of the trial, because of the obvious rigging of evidence and obvious perjury, would have been clear whether the trial had been held at night or at noon. But Luke also has a further, subtler reason for his order, as we will see.

Therefore, the reader should remember that, although the trial segments and the denial segments are printed in parallel lines for purposes of step-by-step comparison in the three versions, the overall placement in Luke is purposefully different from Mark's and Matthew's structure.

The Sanhedrin before whom the trial took place in all three versions was a group of 71 chief priests, elders, and scribes along with the ruling high priest of the year. They decided religious, legal, and internal civic matters for Jews—anything that did not pertain to the Roman law. In judicial processes, defense witnesses were called first and then prosecution witnesses; notice that no defense witnesses are called in any of the three versions.

A. Introduction

MATTHEW 26	MARK 14	LUKE 22
[57]Then those who had seized Jesus led him to Caiaphas, the high priest, where the scribes and the elders had gathered. [58]But Peter followed him at a distance, as far as the courtyard of the high priest, and going inside he sat with the guards to see the end.	[53]And they led Jesus to the high priest; and all the chief priests and the elders and the scribes were assembled. And Peter had followed him at a distance, right into the courtyard of the high priest; and he was sitting with the guards and warming himself at the fire.	[54]Then they seized him and led him away, bringing him into the high priest's house. Peter followed at a distance; [55]and when they had kindled a fire in the middle of the yard and sat down together, Peter sat among them.

1. Mark's simplicity of style is clearly seen (especially if one looks at this passage with the one immediately preceding) by the succession of compound sentences: "and . . . and . . . and." There are hardly any complex sentences or subordinate clauses. But the toughness of his style comes through in that cocky "right into the courtyard."

2. Matthew follows Mark very closely, adding only the grim note "to see the end."

3. Luke also follows Mark closely, although he omits naming the members of the court at this time, holding off until he comes to the trial the next morning. His focus for the moment is not on the trial but on Peter, whom he shows denying Jesus before the trial rather than after it.

The following segment is long. Read Mark through first, then section by section compare Mark and Matthew, then section by section compare Luke with both.

B. The Trial (In Luke, D)

⁵⁹Now the chief priests and the whole council sought false testimony against Jesus that they might put him to death. ⁶⁰But they found none, though many false witnesses came forward.

At last two came forward ⁶¹and said, "This fellow said 'I am able to destroy the temple of God, and to build it in three days.'"

⁶²And the high priest stood up and said "Have you no answer to make? What is it that

⁵⁵Now the chief priests and the whole council sought testimony against Jesus to put him to death; but they found none. ⁵⁶For many bore false witness against him, and their witness did not agree.

⁵⁷And some stood up and bore false witness against him, saying, "We heard him say, 'I will destroy this temple that is made with hands, and in three days I will build another not made with hands.'"

⁵⁹Yet not even so did their testimony agree. ⁶⁰ And the high priest stood up in the midst, and

⁶⁶When day came, the assembly of the elders of the people gathered together, both chief priests and scribes; and they led him away to their council.

these men testify against you?" But Jesus was silent.

asked Jesus, "Have you no answer to make? What is it that these men testify against you?" ⁶⁷But he was silent and made no answer.

And the high priest said to him, "I adjure you by the living God, tell us if you are the Christ, the Son of God."

Again the high priest asked him,

"Are you the Christ, the Son of the Blessed?"

and they said,

⁶⁷If you are the Christ, tell us." But he said to them, "If I tell you, you will not believe; ⁶⁸and if I ask you, you will not answer.

⁶⁴Jesus said to him, "You have said so. But I tell you, hereafter you will see the Son of man seated at the right hand of Power, and coming on the clouds of heaven."

⁶²And Jesus said, "I am;

and you will see the Son of man sitting at the right hand of Power, and coming with the clouds of heaven."

⁶⁹But from now on the Son of man will be seated at the right hand of the Power of God."

⁷⁰And they all said, "Are you the Son of God, then?" And he said to them, "You say that I am."

⁶⁵The high priest tore his robes, and said, "He has uttered blasphemy. Why do we still need witnesses? You have now heard his blasphemy. ⁶⁶What is your judgment?" They answered, "He deserves death."

⁶³And the high priest tore his mantle, and said,

"Why do we still need witnesses? ⁶⁴You have heard his blasphemy. What is your decision?" And they all condemned him as deserving death.

⁷¹And they said,

"What further testimony do we need? We have heard it ourselves from his own lips."

1. Although it is clear in both Mark and Matthew that the high priest had made up their minds beforehand about the outcome of the trial, Mark repeats "false witnesses" in both vv. 56 and 57, hammering it home.

Mark alone specifies the temple made with hands and the temple not made with hands. Symbolically, the first temple means Israel, focused as it was in the temple at Jerusalem; the second temple is the new Church of Christ, the body in which his Spirit would continue to dwell. (It should be noted—again and again—that Mark was writing his narrative long after the

historical events he records, and he was therefore influenced by his knowledge of the very real antagonism between the "two temples" in his own day.)

In contrast to the other two synoptics, Jesus gives a clear affirmative answer in Mark's version to the high priest's questions about his being the Christ: "I am." These words, of course, are a formula most Jews avoided, since it was the way Yahweh had identified himself to Moses. To this day, orthodox Jews will not even write the word "God" but rather "G-d." Yahweh's name—"I am"—was unspeakable, so that when asked a question like "Are you the culprit?" or "Are you called Simon?," a good Jew would use a circumlocution like, "You have said it," or "As you say." (Recall that in John's version of the arrest, when Jesus says, "I am," the Jews fall on the ground in shock at this blasphemous self-assertion.)

Note, too, that in having Jesus' own vigorous admission of who he is at this point, Peter's later denial of who he himself is becomes even more cowardly by contrast. Jesus stands up to the chiefs of his nation, but Peter buckles before maids and bystanders.

In both Mark and Matthew, the high priest recognizes only too well the seemingly blasphemous assertion Jesus makes of himself as well as the obvious reference to the Son of Man we have already seen in the Book of Daniel.

2. Only Matthew gives the name "Caiaphas," and only Matthew has him put Jesus under oath to answer—making his reply even more self-binding to a converted scribe like Matthew. Furthermore, this surely underlines the injustice, since it asks the defendant under oath to incriminate himself.

While Mark's false witnesses quote Jesus as saying "I will destroy the temple," Matthew softens it to "I am able to." This is interesting, especially since most scholars agree that Mark wrote before the actual destruction of the temple and Matthew wrote after.

Although Matthew, the good Hebrew mind, avoids the "I am" by using "You have said so," the rest of the verse leaves no doubt what Jesus was claiming. And, as in Mark, the horror of the high priest underlines that. For those people of our own day who admire Jesus as "a wonderful model, like Mohandas Gandhi," the testimony of this Jewish high priest shows that Jesus himself made a claim far more dramatic than mere moral leadership. There's an irony there somewhere.

3. Luke's order begins to show advantages regarding Peter. Whereas Mark and Matthew show Peter "topping things off" by deserting Jesus even when

he supposedly knows the trial Jesus has been through, Luke has his denials before the bitter experience of the trial.

The most notable thing in Luke's description of the trial is that there are *no* accusations, *no* witnesses, *no* mention of blasphemy, *no* condemnation. Even the identity of the speakers is left as an indefinite "they." The question is: Who are you? It could be a moment from *Oedipus the King.*

Recall, too, the description of the arrest in Luke: This is *the* critical moment, the fullness of time. This question—"Who are you?"—has been hounding Jesus throughout Luke's gospel, from the three temptations in the desert right up to the three taunting temptations from the bystanders at the cross. "Who *are* you?" If you are the Son of God, throw yourself off the temple and you will be saved; if you are the Son of God, come down from the cross.

In the answer to the questions of Jesus' identity, Luke changes the order of the three titles of Mark-Matthew: Christ . . . Son of God (the Blessed) . . . Son of man.

Moreover, unlike Mark and Matthew who say the Jews "will" see Jesus coming as the Son of man in divine power on the clouds (at the end of the world), Luke says "from now on" the Son of man will be seated on a par with the divine power. Luke is not looking so much to the kingdom's fulfillment in the end but at its present and growing reality in the Christian community. The kingdom is about to begin; and as Luke writes, Jesus is already glorified.

In the passage which follows, remember that in Luke's version the mockery comes before Jesus' actual trial (in the morning), whereas in Mark and Matthew it comes as a "natural" result of the condemnation.

C. The Mocking

[67]Then they spat in his face, and struck him; and some slapped him, saying "Prophesy to us, you Christ! Who is it that struck you?"

[65]And some began to spit on him, and to cover his face, and to strike him saying to him "Prophesy!"

And the guards received him with blows.

[63]Now the men who were holding Jesus mocked him and beat him; [64]they also blindfolded him and asked him, "Prophesy! Who is it that struck you?" [65]And they spoke many other words against him reviling him.

1. Mark shows Jesus being mocked first, and only then does he seem to be turned over to the guards who, apparently in their turn, received him and began beating him. This would imply that the initial tormentors were the people spoken of immediately before this in Mark's gospel: the high priests and elders.

2. Matthew dodges this ambiguity by omitting reference to the guards. In Mark and Luke, the "game" is apparently to blindfold their Victim and, since he is a prophet, dare him to say which of them had hit him that time. Matthew, who is usually cautious about such matters, neglects to tell us that the blindfold was put on.

3. Luke, with typical delicacy, spares us the indignity of even suspecting priests guilty of such loathesomeness by saying that it was "the men who were holding Jesus." Nor does he say anything about "spittle," preferring to hide something so disgusting under a vague phrase like "many other words" and "reviling."

D. Peter's Denials and Repentance (B, in Luke)

[69]Now Peter was sitting outside in the courtyard. And a maid came up to him, and said, "You also were with Jesus the Galilean." [70]But he denied it before them all, saying, "I do not know what you mean."

[66]And as Peter was below in the courtyard, one of the maids of the high priest came; [67]and seeing Peter warming himself, she looked at him and said, "You also were with the Nazarene, Jesus." But he denied it, saying, "I neither know nor understand what you mean."

[56]Then a maid, seeing him as he sat in the light and gazing at him,

said, "This man also was with him." [57]But he denied it, saying, "Woman, I do not know him."

[61]And when he went out to the porch, another maid saw him, and she said to the bystanders, "This man was with Jesus of Nazareth." And again he denied it with an oath, "I do not know the man."

And he went out into the gateway. [69]And the maid saw him, and began again to say to the bystanders, "This man is one of them." [70]But again he denied it.

[58]And a little later someone else saw him and said, "You also are one of them." But Peter said, "Man I am not!"

[73]After a little while the bystanders came up and

And after a little while again the bystanders

[59]And after an interval of about an hour still an-

said to Peter, "Certainly you are also one of them, for your accent betrays you."

⁷⁴Then he began to invoke a curse on himself and to swear, "I do not know the man!" And immediately the cock crowed.

⁷⁵And Peter remembered the saying of Jesus, "Before the cock crows, you will deny me three times." And he went out and wept bitterly.

said to Peter, "Certainly you are one of them; for you are a Galilean. ⁷¹But he began to invoke a curse on himself and to swear, "I do not know this man of whom you speak!" And immediately the cock crowed a second time.

And Peter remembered how Jesus had said to him, "Before the cock crows twice, you will deny me three times." And he broke down and wept.

other insisted, saying, "Certainly this man also was with him; for he is a Galilean."

⁶⁰But Peter said, "Man, I do not know what you are saying." And immediately, while he was still speaking, the cock crowed.

⁶¹And the Lord turned and looked at Peter. And Peter remembered the word of the Lord, how he had said to him, "Before the cock crows today, you will deny me three times." ⁶²And he went out and wept bitterly.

1. Notice how Mark makes a typical careless "Markism" when the cock crows for the second time, and Mark has not bothered to tell us it crowed the first time!

A touch of Greek makes the end of Mark's version of the scene much more vital. *Epibalōn eklaien* can better be translated, "He threw himself down and wept and wept."

2. Matthew builds a climax better than Mark. In his version Peter is accosted first by one maid, then another, then by all the bystanders. And it is only Matthew who gives a legitimate reason why the bystanders would immediately know Peter was not a native of Jerusalem. (This segment, among many other reasons, convinces scholars that although both Matthew and Luke knew Mark's version and used it, neither knew of the other's version. This dramatic buildup and the concrete reason for unmasking Peter would have appealed to Luke and, had he known of Matthew's version, he surely would have used it.)

3. Luke, again with his delicate concern for both Peter and Jesus, says nothing about swearing.

He also heightens the dramatic impact of the scene's climax by having the cock crow, "while he was still speaking."

But the most memorable detail which Luke inserts is the chilling: "And the Lord turned and looked at Peter." Whether Jesus actually was being brought by at that moment (in Luke's version on his way to the morning trial) or not is hardly important. Luke has far more important things to do than concentrate on accurate reportage.

Recall the passage, in Luke only, at the Last Supper: "Simon, Simon, behold, Satan demanded to have you, that he might sift you like wheat, but I have prayed for you that your faith may not fail; and when you have *turned* again, strengthen your brethren." Immediately, Peter began to defend himself and swear he would go to prison and even death with Jesus. At that moment, Luke says Jesus predicted this triple denial before the cock crowed. When the event occurs in the courtyard, Jesus turns to Peter and Peter turns to see him.

The Hebrew word for "conversion"—like the Latin and Greek words for "conversion"—is the word "to turn back," to get back to the right way of doing things. The recent Byrds' recording of "Turn, Turn, Turn" is based on an Old Testament text. It is consistent in both Isaiah (in Hebrew) and Luke (in Greek) that the Lord must first turn toward us (*strephein*, like the Latin *vertere*, "turn") before we can turn back toward him (*epistraphein*, like the Latin *convertere*, "return").

Throughout his gospel, Luke has made a special effort to picture Peter as the "model disciple," a mixture of belief and fear, relying on the Lord and coming back to begin over even after he has sinned.

Just as Peter is the focal character of Luke's gospel, Paul is the focal character of Luke's Acts of the Apostles. Both are "converts" in this two-volume work of Luke—Peter with this shattering experience in the courtyard, Paul with his shattering experience on the road to Damascus. In both cases, the Lord turns first and they, with awesome realization, turn wholly to him.

Notice, too, that Jesus is not angry when he turns. He had, after all, predicted this—and the prediction of a prophet is an expression of the will of God, even when it is painful to the prophet himself.

It is somewhat easier now to see why Luke might have put this scene before Jesus' trial rather than after it. This event surely deprives him of his last friend, but—like the mother in labor—Jesus knows that this pain from Peter and the pain to come will bear fruit when the kingdom comes.

SUMMARY OF DIFFERENT EMPHASES

Mark

Mark is typically assertive: Jesus says forthrightly, "I am," even at the risk of confounding Jews who would never use those words. As is common with Mark, the Good News is meant to shock. Nor does he shy away from showing his friend, Peter, the first pope, denying with oaths that he even knew Jesus—within hours of his own first communion, his ordination as a priest, and his first Mass. It was not an easy-going, one-hour-a-week Christian community Mark was writing for; they were under threat at every minute from Roman prisons and martyrdom. Even the first pope gave in to the enemy. But he was forgiven, and he died a martyr only a year or two before Mark's gospel was written and in the very city where his gospel circulated.

Matthew

In this segment, too, Matthew's Jewish training and sensibilities come through. He knows the name of the high priest, he knows the need of witnesses, but he does not hesitate to underline the illegality of the trial by putting it at night and showing that no defense witnesses were allowed. Like any other Jew, he hesitates to use "I am," the name of God, and, like any other Jew, he draws back from picturing the chief priests spitting at Jesus and striking him—which Mark finds not difficult at all.

Luke

Luke's version of the trial is the barest: there are no accusations, no witnesses, no mention of blasphemy, no condemnation. The whole thing hinges on who Jesus is. When he answers that question, the trial is over. Unlike Matthew and Mark, he does not see Jesus in the apocalyptic terms of Daniel, coming to power only in the end time. "From now on" the Son of Man will share the power of Yahweh. Also, for Luke's audience the Roman trial was probably the only important, "official" one.

But the most striking difference in Luke is his switching of the trial and Peter's denials from Mark's original order. In the first place, Luke's ordering of events evades the obvious illegality of a night trial, which the elders would

probably not have risked with a person they wanted to get out of the way as much as they did Jesus. The temper of the people who had greeted Jesus with *hosannahs* the previous Sunday was too volatile for that.

Secondly, the "desertion" by Peter leaves Jesus more dramatically abandoned at the beginning of the trial. This most ardent disciple—with whom the weak Christian reader can so easily identify—allows the reader to "get into Peter's shoes" and see what abandoning Jesus is like. Moreover, Peter's denials are given so much stress in homilies that it is easy to forget that, for all his bluster and failings, Peter was at least not hiding out with the others in the upper room. He did not pass the test in the courtyard, but at least he was courageous (or foolhardy) enough not to run away from the test as the others had done.

Finally, with his customary kindness, Luke disassociates Peter from "the bad guys" by having not only his denial but his conversion occur before the mockery of Jesus by his captors and the travesty of justice at his trial. However, Luke's version is still a slower and more literary stripping-away of one support after another from Jesus—as one finds in Greek drama.

SUMMARY OF SIMILARITIES

(1) Although Luke purposefully reverses the Peter section and the trial section, the development of events within each section is relatively the same.

(2) Although in Luke the outcome of the trial is not as explicitly a foregone conclusion and although there are no false witnesses, the pivotal question is whether Jesus is the Christ. In all three, Jesus says that he is. When he does that, the trial is over.

(3) In all three gospels, there is an intentional and bitter irony of situation: Jesus, who is regal in his ability to rise up above his treatment, is on trial on precisely those grounds: his kingship. And his condemnation is at the hands of leaders and priests, who condemn him in the name of God.

(4) In all three, even in Luke who shies from such ugliness, Jesus is mocked and beaten and told to prophesy.

(5) All four evangelists, even John, agree that Peter's denials occurred at night. He is challenged three separate times and each time renounces his faith in Jesus publicly. The cock crows, he remembers Jesus' warning, and he repents with bitter tears.

(6) Jesus' silence in this trial and in the trial with Pilate has two purposes. First, at the time the gospels were written, all communications between the

Jewish community and the Christian community had broken down. Orthodox Jews were even turning Christians into the civil authorities as members of a new religion which perverted true Judaism—which the Romans tolerated. In these trials, there is an example of that breakdown in communications right from the start, as well as an example to those who themselves were to be handed over by their fellow Jews to the Roman authorities and condemned to death. It shows how the first Christians reacted to a trial which many of the first readers of these gospels would themselves be called to undergo.

Secondly, though, Jesus' silence was also the will of God, expressed to him and to the Jewish nation in prophecies about how Yahweh would treat his anointed: "Harshly dealt with, he bore it humbly; he never opened his mouth, like a lamb that is led to the slaughterhouse; like a sheep that is dumb before its shearers, never opening its mouth." Isaiah 53 is only one of many passages like this, but it is worth reading as a foreshadowing of this most critical weekend in the life of mankind.

8

THE ROMAN TRIAL

As in the Jewish trial, all three evangelists telescope events in the trial before Pilate. Any dramatic presentation of a trial does the same thing (e.g., Perry Mason). We are generally spared such details as the selection of a jury, swearing in, etc., in order to focus on the more important aspects of the proceedings, especially the climax. Here, too, the more important factor is not the details of the process but the pressures that determined the outcome of the process: the tensions Pilate faced with Jesus' evident innocence on the one side and the Jewish leaders' threatening insistence on the other.

The outlines are again parallel, but there are insertions by Matthew and Luke and a different structuring of the materials within the segments; all of these changes from Mark's outline are purposeful. (And notice that Mark wraps up the episode in 15 verses, where Matthew gives it 26 verses and Luke gives it 24.)

Outline

MATTHEW	MARK	LUKE
A. Morning; Jesus to Pilate	A. Morning; Jesus to Pilate	A. Morning; Jesus to Pilate

B. Death of Judas		B. Charge of treason
C. Jesus questioned	C. Jesus questioned	C. Jesus questioned; declared innocent; repetition of treason.
		D. Jesus to Herod; declared innocent; repetition of treason
E. Offer of Barabbas; Pilate's wife's dream	E. Offer of Barabbas	
F. Choice of Barabbas	F. Choice of Barabbas	F. Choice of Barabbas
G. "Crucify him!"	G. "Crucify him!"	G. "Crucify him!"
H. Pilate's hand washing		
I. Barabbas released; Jesus handed over.	I. Barabbas released; Jesus handed over.	I. Barabbas released; Jesus handed over.

A. Morning: Jesus Sent to Pilate

MATTHEW 27	MARK 15	LUKE 23
[1]When morning came, all the chief priests and the elders of the people took counsel against Jesus to put him to death; [2]and they bound him and led him away	[1]And as soon as it was morning the chief priests, with the elders and scribes, and the whole council held a consultation; and they bound Jesus and led him away.	
and delivered him to Pilate, the governor.	and delivered him to Pilate.	[1]Then the whole company of them arose, and brought him before Pilate.

1. Mark and Matthew make some small attempt to put a touch of legality on the proceedings by having this morning "consultation." Even though the actual trial had been, illegally, at night, the official decision was made in the morning. Luke, who has put the trial itself in the morning, simply goes on to the next step.

Note again how Mark very simply strings events together with no other transition but "and."

B. The Death of Judas (Matthew only)

³When Judas, his betrayer, saw that he was condemned he repented and brought back the thirty pieces of silver to the chief priests and elders, ⁴ saying, "I have sinned in betraying innocent blood." They said, "What is that to us? See to it yourself." ⁵And throwing down the pieces of silver in the temple, he departed; and he went and hanged himself. ⁶But the chief priests, taking the pieces of silver, said, "It is not lawful to put them into the treasury since they are blood money." ⁷So they took counsel, and bought with them the potter's field, to bury strangers in. ⁸Therefore, that field has been called the Field of Blood to this day. ⁹Then was fulfilled what had been spoken by the prophet Jeremiah, saying, "And they took the thirty pieces of silver, the price of him on whom a price had been set by some of the sons of Israel, ¹⁰and they gave them for the potter's field, as the Lord directed me."

1. The death of Judas itself seems incidental to this insertion. (One Greek

word.) The emphasis is rather on the silver (used four times itself and referred to by "it" three times) and on the price of blood (three times).

Why insert it here, since it can't possibly be in chronological sequence— how can the chief priests be with Pilate and with Judas at the same time?

There most probably was a "potter's field" (the better translation is probably "treasury's field") near Jerusalem where strangers were buried and which was called "The Field of Blood." We have seen earlier in this book how past cultures spun etiological tales to explain how things got the way they are or how they got their names. But Matthew has a far larger purpose here than a historical process of tracing the name of a burial plot back to the time of Jesus.

For Matthew, the insistence on "the price of blood" emphasizes the whole tone of these trials. It is only in Matthew (27:25) that, when Pilate washes his hands of the case, the Jews call out that grisly challenge, "His blood be on us and on our children!" That sentence is the whole point of the scene, and Matthew, who is not writing history but trying to explain it, inserts this episode of Judas to put the event of Jesus' condemnation in the full perspective of history. The Jewish leaders, like Judas, have the blood of an innocent man on their hands. But Judas and then Pilate refuse to continue the responsibility for such an injustice, leaving the Jews alone to carry the burden—which they willingly do, according to Matthew.

On the other hand, no matter what the guilt of the Jewish leaders who incite the crowds to ask for Barabbas and call for Jesus' death, they cannot overturn the plan of Jesus and his Father which was revealed throughout Jewish history. Just as Judas is a pawn in the hands of the Jewish leaders, the Jewish leaders themselves are pawns in the hands of the enemy. Their very act of "buying God" with blood money was predicted by the prophet Zechariah (not Jeremiah): "But God told me, 'Throw into the treasury this princely sum at which they have valued me.' Taking the 30 shekels of silver, I threw them into the Temple of Yahweh." (Zech 11:13) (Matthew was doubtless quoting from memory.)

Did Zechariah foresee Judas photographically? Or is Matthew recording a historical event? Very likely not. But both did know the ways of Yahweh, and Yahweh was preparing Israel for its Messiah. Matthew (or his sources) knew of (1) the passage in Zechariah, (2) the betrayal of the Messiah by Judas—and by the Jewish leaders, (3) most important, the meaning of this event in the light of God's dealings with his people over the ages.

C. Jesus Is Questioned

MATTHEW | MARK | LUKE

LUKE

²And they began to accuse him saying, "We found this man perverting our nation, and forbidding us to give tribute to Caesar, and saying that he himself is Christ, a king."

MATTHEW

¹¹Now Jesus stood before the governor; and the governor asked him, "Are you the King of the Jews?" Jesus said to him, "You have said so."

¹²But when he was accused by the chief priests and elders, he made no answer. ¹³Then Pilate said to him, "Do you not hear how many things they testify against you?" ¹⁴But he gave them no answer, not even to a single charge; so that the governor wondered greatly.

MARK

²And Pilate asked him, "Are you the King of the Jews?" And he answered him, "You have said so."

³And the chief priests accused him of many things.
⁴And Pilate asked him, "Have you no answer to make? See how many charges they bring against you." ⁵But Jesus made no further answer, so that Pilate wondered.

LUKE

⁴And Pilate said to the chief priests and the multitudes, "I find no crime in this man." ⁵But they were urgent, saying, "He stirs up the people, teaching throughout all Judea, from Galilee even to this place."

1. Mark (and Matthew) start off slam-bang in the middle of the trial, without even an accusation to Pilate. Mark, writing for Romans, probably didn't

need to mention who Pilate was or what his office was. But the Jews deliver him, and right away Pilate asks, "Are you the King of the Jews?"—which incidentally had been no part of the previous evening's accusations. Once Jesus admits (with the Jewish avoidance of "I am") that he is indeed the King of the Jews, the chief priests accuse him of "many things." The whole thing is a charade anyway, and Mark wants to get it over with. The pagan Pilate wonders, but the Jews—despite their knowledge of their Scriptures—do not.

2. Matthew constantly stresses that Pilate is the governor (four times already in the chapter). Other than that, he has a remarkable similarity to Mark.

3. Luke, throughout the Roman trial, has a clearer-cut structure. Alone of the three evangelists, Luke has the accusation loud and clear before Pilate asks any questions: The charge is not blasphemy but treason. Despite what Jesus himself had preached (Luke 20:25 and parallels) about rendering to Caesar the things that are Caesar's they charge him with forbidding Jews to give tribute. This further underlines the deceitfulness of the chief priests. But it also stands out in stark contrast to Pilate's official declaration: "I find no crime in this man," which he will repeat three more times before Luke's treatment of the scene is over. (Remember, too, that Luke is writing for a Gentile audience.) But despite Pilate's judgment, the priests and the "multitudes" shout again that Jesus is a poltiical revolutionary and has been stirring up all Judea, from a base in Galilee.

The reference to Galilee, which was under the jurisdiction of the puppet Jewish king, Herod, gives Pilate what he thinks may be an "out."

D. Jesus Is Sent to Herod (Luke only)

⁶When Pilate heard this, he asked whether the man was a Galilean. ⁷And when he learned that he belonged to Herod's jurisdiction, he sent him over to Herod, who was himself in Jerusalem at that time. ⁸When Herod saw Jesus, he was very glad, for he had long desired to see him, because he had heard

about him, and he was hoping to see some sign done by him. [9]So he questioned him at some length; but he made no answer. [10]The chief priests and the scribes stood by, vehemently accusing him. [11]And Herod with his soldiers treated him with contempt and mocked him; then, arraying him in gorgeous apparel, he sent him back to Pilate. [12]And Herod and Pilate became friends with each other that very day, for before this they had been at enmity with each other.

1. Galilee had been a staging area for guerilla uprisings for a long time, as such barren hill country so frequently is for occupied peoples. Herod, the puppet king of Galilee, is mentioned only once in Matthew and only twice in Mark, but he is mentioned six times in Luke's gospel and twice in Luke's Acts of the Apostles.

This is the same Herod who beheaded John the Baptist, who had been Jesus' friend. He is the same Herod who, some Pharisees told Jesus, was trying to kill Jesus, too. He is the same Herod whom Jesus called "that fox."

Two of Luke's references may indicate his sources for this and other details about Herod. In Acts 13:1, he mentioned Manaen, an elder of the church in Antioch who had grown up with Herod; some scholars suspect that Luke may have written in Antioch. In Luke 8:3, he mentions Joanna, the wife of Chusa, who was Herod's steward; only Luke mentions that this Joanna was one of the women who followed Jesus and was at his tomb. Either or both of these people could have been the source of this episode in Luke, which the other two evangelists seem to have been unaware of.

Why does Luke insert it here? For one reason, it might very well be historical. For another, it emphasizes still further the Gentile Pilate's attempts to avoid condemning Jesus. Remember, too, that Luke's readers had never heard this story before and, as a storyteller, Luke knew this possibility of the

hero finding a way out would increase the suspense, especially since the hero is so manifestly innocent.

Mark later has the Roman soldiers put a mock king costume on Jesus, and Luke here has the Jewish king do that.

Furthermore, this Herod seems very well caricaturized in *Jesus Christ Superstar*—an effete, overindulged Eastern monarch looking for diversion, a magic trick, from this reputed miracle worker. Like his people, he is asking for a "sign"—and doesn't see that Jesus is the sign of the Suffering Servant of Yahweh, standing right in front of him.

While Jesus responds to Pilate's questions, he is completely silent here. According to the Book of Wisdom (8:12), even the powerful must wait for a wise man in his silence. Sirach 20:1 says that the wise man remains silent in the face of rebuke that is uncalled for, while the fool "multiplies words." (The Roman writer Martial put it more clearly: "There is no glory in excelling a donkey.")

At any rate, Herod cannot condemn Jesus and sends him back to Pilate, who also cannot condemn him. Luke thus has his biblical requirement of two witnesses, officially testifying to Jesus' innocence.

"Herod and Pilate became friends." Apparently there had been a feud between them, and perhaps Herod takes this recognition of his authority as a kind of peace offering from Pilate—which is ironic, considering that Pilate was trying to get rid of a hot potato.

Later in Acts, Luke tells of the prayer offered by the community after the elders of the synagogue had released Peter and John. They begin quoting Genesis and draw a conclusion about Jerusalem, Herod, and Pilate:

> "Kings on earth setting out to war, princes making an alliance against the Lord, and against his anointed." This is what has come true: in this very city, Herod and Pontius Pilate made an alliance between the pagan nations and the peoples of Israel, against your holy servant Jesus, whom you anointed, but only to bring about the very thing that you in your strength and wisdom had predetermined should happen. (Acts 4:26–27)

E. The Sentence of Death

MATTHEW	MARK	LUKE
		[13]Pilate then called together the chief priests and the rulers and the people, [14]and said to

them, "You brought me this man as one who was perverting the people; and after examining him before you, behold, I did not find this man guilty of any of your charges against him; ¹⁵neither did Herod, for he sent him back to us. Behold, nothing deserving of death has been done by him; ¹⁶I will therefore chastise him and release him.

¹⁵Now at the feast the governor was accustomed to release for the crowd any one prisoner whom they wanted. ¹⁶And they had then a notorious prisoner called Barabbas. ¹⁷So when they had gathered, Pilate said to them, "Whom do you want me to release for you, Barabbas or Jesus who is called Christ?" ¹⁸For he knew that it was out of envy that they had delivered him up.

¹⁷Besides, while he was sitting on the judgment seat, his wife sent word to him, "Have nothing to do with that righteous man, for I have suffered much over him today in a dream."

⁶Now at the feast he used to release for them one prisoner whom they asked.

⁷And among the rebels in prison, who had committed murder in the insurrection, there was a man called Barabbas. ⁸And the crowd came up and began to ask Pilate to do as he was used to do for them. ⁹And he answered them, "Do you want me to release for you the King of the Jews?" ¹⁰For he perceived that it was out of envy that the chief priests had delivered him up.

[20]Now the chief priests and the elders persuaded the people to ask for Barabbas and destroy Jesus. [21]The governor again said to them, "Which of the two do you want me to release for you?" And they said, "Barabbas." [22]Pilate said to them, "Then what shall I do with Jesus who is called Christ?" They all said, "Let him be crucified." And he said, "Why? What evil has he done?" But they shouted all the more, "Let him be crucified." [24]So when Pilate saw that he was gaining nothing, but rather that a riot was beginning, he took water and washed his hands before the crowd, saying "I am innocent of this man's blood, see to it yourselves." [25]And all the people answered "His blood be on us and on our children!"	[11]But the chief priests stirred up the crowd to have him release for them Barabbas instead. [12]And Pilate again said to them, "Then what shall I do with the man whom you call the King of the Jews?" [13]And they cried out again, "Crucify him." [14]And Pilate said to them, "Why? What evil has he done?" But they shouted all the more "Crucify him."	[18]But they all cried out together, "Away with this man, and release to us Barabbas"—[19]a man who had been thrown into prison for an insurrection started in the city, and for murder. [20]Pilate addressed them once more, desiring to release Jesus: [21]but they shouted out, "Crucify, crucify him!" [22]A third time he said to them, "Why? What evil has he done?" I have found in him no crime deserving death; I will therefore chastise him and release him." But they were urgent, demanding with loud cries that he should be crucified. And their voices prevailed.
[26]Then he released for them Barabbas and having scourged Jesus, delivered him to be crucified.	[15]So Pilate, wishing to satisfy the crowd, released for them Barabbas; and having scourged Jesus, he delivered him to be crucified.	[24]So Pilate gave sentence that their demand should be granted. [25]He released the man who had been thrown into prison for insurrection and murder, whom they asked for; but Jesus he delivered up to their will.

1. Mark is again expeditious. Pilate has a very small role here, in contrast to the uses that both Matthew and Luke put him to. Perceiving their envious

motives, he offers them Jesus as his regular Passover amnesty. He argues when they ask for Barabbas, but they shout him down and—crowd-pleaser as Mark sees him—he gives in.

2. Matthew follows Mark's text except for three dramatic liberties.

Most critics agree that the intervention of Pilate's wife and her dream are a legend Matthew has heard about the tiral, one he uses to dramatic effect, offering Pilate one more motive for interfering in the priests' plans. (According to the Jewish historian Josephus, the historical Pilate was surely not a man renowned for kindliness and caution!) Matthew also has used dreams in his infancy narratives..

Pilate's symbolic handwashing is another way of underlining this man's "innocence" and therefore the treachery of the Jewish leaders. And it also fits the pattern Matthew has set up with the thirty pieces of silver being the price of this man's blood. Matthew has used this reference to shedding the blood of the prophets before, in the woes Jesus has called down on the scribes and Pharisees earlier:

"Alas for you, scribes and Pharisees, you hypocrites! You who build sepulchers of the prophets and decorate the tombs of holy men, saying, 'We would never have joined in shedding the blood of the prophets, had we lived in our fathers' day.' So! Your own evidence tells against you! You are the sons of those who murdered the prophets! Very well, then, finish off the work that your fathers began." (Matt. 23:29–32)

The manner in which the Jews—and Matthew is careful to say "all the people"—call this blood down on themselves and on their children is chilling. It is ironic that at this Passover, which celebrated the feast whereby the Israelites sprinkled the blood of the lamb on their doorposts in Egypt to elude the angel of death, they should be calling down upon themselves the guilt for the blood of the Lamb of God—who had come to help them elude death. The cause for this heavy assertion was very probably Matthew's realization that in 70 A.D. the Jews were dispossessed of their capital and that he saw it as a direct punishment for what their leaders had done there to Jesus.

3. Whereas the other two begin the trial with an abrupt question from Pilate, Luke prefaces it with a more realistic statement of charges: (1) perverting the nation, (2) forbidding tribute, (3) claiming kingship—in effect, civil treason. And he hammers this home explicitly again and again throughout the remainder of his version of the trial. One of his major purposes, after all, is to convince his Gentile audience that Jesus was a spiritual not a political

revolutionary. Three times Pilate explicitly and formally says he has found no crime in this man. Twice he has offered to chastise Jesus instead of crucifying him. (It is subtly ironic that he says he finds no crime in Jesus and *therefore* will chastise him.)

Luke has three repetitions of the charges and three definite statements from Pilate about Jesus' innocence: First Pilate declares *"I find no crime in this man"* (23:4). Was it perhaps a legal formula he was repeating? In any event, he later states: *"I do not find this man guilty of any of your charges against him. Neither did Herod. Nothing deserving death has been done by him"* (vv. 14–15). And, finally, he says *"I have found no crime in him deserving death"* (v. 22, which Luke explicitly states is Pilate's *third* attempt).

Notice too that Luke underlines Pilate's motive in v. 20, "desiring to release Jesus." Notice also that at the return from Herod, Pilate summons only "the chief priests and rulers," not "the multitudes."

In all three it is heavily ironic that the Jews bring Jesus to Pilate on the charges of being a treasonous revolutionary and yet scream for a treasonous revolutionary—and murderer—in his stead. But it is Luke who inserts a repetition of Barabbas' treacheries at the very time of Jesus' sentencing.

There is an ironic pun, too, in Barabbas' name. In Hebrew, "bar" means "son," as in Simon bar Jonah; "abba" means "father" and it is the word Jesus used himself about Yahweh, "Abba, Father." It is ironic that Barabbas is chosen instead of the Son of the Father.

Even in tiny touches, Luke stresses the guilt of the Jewish leaders over the guilt of the Roman leader. It was not Pilate who offered Barabbas but the Jews' own idea. And where Matthew and Mark say that Pilate "delivered him to be crucified," Luke specifies it with "Jesus he delivered up to their [the Jewish leaders] will.

SUMMARY OF DIFFERENT EMPHASES

Mark

Mark is typically terse, only two-thirds the length of either of the other synoptics. He is abrupt as well, starting out right in the middle of the trial without any witnesses. If he knows about the death of Judas or the questioning by Herod, he doesn't mention it. And yet by his very brevity and abruptness, he somehow underlines the callousness of the people involved even more than the other evangelists who take more time with details.

Matthew

Matthew is more studied. He obviously has a theme of blood-guilt running through this whole section: first Judas, then Pilate, then the "people." But at least Judas and Pilate make some inept attempt at disassociating themselves from their guilt. The Jews are left with it, to their peril.

Luke

Luke is the most studied of the three. He is careful to have the charges announced, and careful to have Pilate deny the charges three distinct times, each time in an official tone. He also joins Herod, the puppet Jewish king, with Pilate in finding no fault in this man. Notice too that from the time Jesus is returned from Herod, unlike Mark and Matthew, the only Jewish characters other than Jesus in the scene are "the chief priests and elders of the people" (v. 13)—not the Jewish people as a whole. Nor does he have the chief priests incite "the people" to shout for crucifixion, as Mark and Matthew do. Matthew takes great care to remove the principal guilt first from Judas and then from the Roman governor; then he puts it squarely on the entire Jewish nation. Luke is not so wholesale; he puts the guilt squarely on the leaders. The scene is spare, like a Greek play: Pilate could be Creon, Jesus the condemned Oedipus, and the elders the Greek chorus. But for Luke, the Jewish people as a whole are innocent and so still fit subjects for the message.

SUMMARY OF SIMILARITIES

(1) The actors are generally the same (with the exception of Judas, Herod, Pilate's wife—and significantly in Luke, the absence of "the people"). The time is morning: the elders of the people hold a consultation and take Jesus off to Pilate.

(2) Pilate asks Jesus if he is the King of the Jews—each understanding something different by those words—and Jesus answers equivalently that he is. In all three, both the question and the answer are verbally identical. All three play on the loaded word "king," which could mean a purely religious messiah or a real threat to Caesar's power. (John will make it even more specific when he has the crowd cry out, "We have no king but Caesar!") In all three, Jesus' answer leaves the interpretation of the loaded word to Pilate

who, by his subsequent actions with the crowd, surely seems to believe Jesus is not a political threat to Caesar.

(3) It is interesting to note that from his response to Pilate's first question Jesus does not utter another word until he has begun his trek to Calvary.

(4) In all three, Pilate releases a known revolutionary and murderer named Barabbas instead of a man he knows is falsely accused of being a revolutionary. Three times Pilate tries to dissuade them, and in his third attempt all three statements are verbally identical. Finally, Pilate gives in to the crowd and sends Jesus to be first scourged, then crucified.

9

CRUCIFIXION AND DEATH

"LONG LIVE THE KING!"

Lest we get lost in details, checking small and large differences from text to text, recall that the passion account is an organic part of the whole gospel message—in fact its climax and fulfillment, both historical and historic. The core of that message of Jesus is the proclamation of the kingdom—a totally new "world," completely counter to the accepted values of worldings, even to the values of many dedicated and sincere Jews. Jesus has been edging toward this moment, this fulfillment, all through the gospel story: "It is at hand." He had warned, as we saw, that the coming of the kingdom would not be "a sign to be observed," like the symbolic signs in the Book of Daniel. It would be "in the midst of you," a spiritual change, a *metanoia*, a con-version, a complete about-face of one's values. And surely the kingdom inaugurated by Jesus' passion is like no earthly kingdom.

As we saw, Jesus' parables and proverbs and preaching were all warning that entrance into the kingdom would mean a total reversal of one's previous values. In pages heavy with irony, the three evangelists underscore this "reversal message." If irony is a figurative means to say exactly the opposite of what one really intends, it is the perfect vehicle for the Christian message. Here is your king! He is poor, outcast, condemned, deserted. He is a king

whose crown is made of thorns, and whose throne is a gibbet. It is a picture to confound the mind, a scandal to Jews and madness to Greeks. No wonder that he is a confusion to literalists. No wonder that he is a threat to materialists. The wonder is that pale agnostics can still dare to say, "What a nice man. What a fine model for conduct." The conduct he calls for if one is to find his kingdom, as he does here, is an utter reversal of what one now thinks is truly important.

Outline

Because Matthew follows Mark with such remarkable closeness, we can treat the two together.

MATTHEW AND MARK

LUKE

A. Mockery by the Roman soldiers
B. The Crucifixion
   —Simon of Cyrene

   —The crucifixion
   —Division of Jesus' garments

B. The Crucifixion
   —Simon of Cyrene
   —The women of Jerusalem
   —The crucifixion (with two others)
   —Division of Jesus' garments; "Father, forgive."

C. The Vigil
   —Inscription; Drink
   —Two fellow criminals
   —Derision by
      —passersby
      —priests

   —two robbers

C. The Vigil

   —Derision by

      —The rulers
      —Soldiers (inscription; drink)
      —Two criminals
         —The Good Thief

D. The Death
   —Darkness: noon to three

   —"My God, My God!"
   —Death
   —Curtain
   —Centurion
   —Women

D. The Death
   —Darkness: noon to three
   —Curtain
   —"Father, into thy hands!"
   —Death

   —Centurion
   —Women

The Mockery

MATTHEW 27

[27]Then the soldiers of the governor took Jesus into the praetorium, and they gathered the whole battalion before him. [28]And they stripped him and put a scarlet robe upon him, [29]and braiding a crown of thorns they put it on his head, and put a reed in his right hand. And kneeling before him they mocked him, saying, "Hail, King of the Jews!" [3]And they spat upon him, and took the reed and struck him on the head. [31]And when they had mocked him, they stripped him of the robe, and put his own clothes on him, and led him away to crucify him.

MARK 15

[16]And the soldiers led him away inside the palace (that is, the praetorium); and they called together the whole battalion. [17]And they clothed him in a purple cloak, and braiding a crown of thorns they put it on him. [18]And they began to salute him, "Hail, King of the Jews!" [19]And they struck his head with a reed, and spat upon him, and they knelt down in homage to him. [20]And when they had mocked him, they stripped him of the purple cloak, and put his own clothes on him. And they led him out to crucify him.

1. The only noticeable difference between the two is that Mark speaks of purple cloak (suggesting imperial robes) and Matthew, probably more correctly, changes it to the scarlet cloak which Roman legionaries wore. Purple was a color reserved for royalty, but the purpose of this ironic investiture is the same for both.

2. The scourging which preceded this event was not the "chastising" of Luke's version (a light beating as a warning for bad boys) but a beating with metal-tipped whips.

The praetorium both speak of was the headquarters of the Roman soldiers. The thorns would be the long thorns used for fires, and probably stored in the courtyard. These probably could have been woven into a circlet like the radiate crowns of Greek kings, similar to the one on our Statute of Liberty.

The mockery is a parody of the acclaim given to an emperor after a victory. To the soldiers Jesus appears to be only another prisoner and a means to wile away the time in a bit of sadistic horseplay: If you want to be a king, we'll make you one! Their "game" expresses their contempt not only for this so-called king, but also for the people he "rules," whose little uprisings plague the lives of these soldiers.

Ironically, Jesus is actually proclaimed a king when he really is at the brink of fulfilling his kingly duty of inaugurating his kingdom.

3. Although he knows of this incident from his copy of Mark, Luke omits the incident entirely. First of all, he has already had a mockery in Herod's court, and he wants his readers to realize that the blame was on the Jewish leadership and not on the Romans. Moreover, it is typical of him to spare Jesus the worst indignities if he can.

B. The Crucifixion

MATTHEW	MARK	LUKE
[32]As they were marching out, they came upon a man of Cyrene, Simon by name; this man they compelled to carry his cross.	[21]And they compelled a passer-by, Simon of Cyrene, who was coming in from the country, the father of Alexander and Rufus to carry his cross.	[26]And as they led him away, they seized on Simon of Cyrene, who was coming in from the country, and laid on him the cross, to carry it behind Jesus. [27]And there followed him a great multitude of the people, and of women who bewailed and lamented him. [28]But Jesus turning to them said, "Daughters of Jerusalem, do not weep for me, but weep for yourselves and for your children. [29]For behold, the days are coming when they will say, 'Blessed are the barren and the wombs that never bore, and the breasts that never gave suck!' [30]Then they will begin to say to the mountains 'Fall on us'; and to the hills, 'Cover us.' [31]For if they do this when the wood is green, what will happen when it is dry?" [32]Two others also, who were criminals, were led away to be put to death with him.

³³And when they came to a place called Golgotha (which means the place of a skull), ³⁴they offered him wine to drink, mingled with gall; but when he tasted it, he would not drink it. And when they had crucified him [See v. 38] they divided his garments among them by casting lots; ³⁶then they sat down and kept watch over him there,

²²And they brought him to the place called Golgotha (which means the place of a skull). And they offered him wine mingled with myrrh but he did not take it.

And they crucified him [See v. 27] and divided his garments among them, casting lots for them, to decide what each should take.

³³And when they came to the place which is called The Skull there they crucified him, and the criminals, one on the right and one on the left. ³⁴And Jesus said, "Father, forgive them; for they know not what they do." And they cast lots to divide his garments. ³⁵And the people stood by, watching.

1. Mark and Matthew are again almost verbally identical.

Simon of Cyrene is a puzzling character, coming as he does practically from nowhere, and yet with a known home town and with two sons. Cyrene is in North Africa near what is now Bengasi in Libya. Perhaps he was an emigrated Jew visiting the center of Judaism for Passover. It is suggested that he must have been converted, since his sons are known to Mark and presumably to his Roman audience. Matthew and Luke, however, writing in different places and for different audiences omitted their unknown names.

Normally the condemned prisoner carried only the crossbar of his cross, since the upright beam was a permanent fixture at the place of execution. But very likely, after the scourging with leaded whips, Jesus was weaker than his two fellow victims. Simon is a model of Christian discipleship, ready to help Jesus carry the burden of his cross and to share his sufferings. Simon is willing literally to "take up my cross and follow me."

The Aramaic word *gulgulta* means "skull," and the form we have is an attempt to render it into Greek. The Latin word for "skull" is *calvaria*, hence our word "Calvary." It is a grisly detail which all three share—though Luke bypasses the Aramaic approximation. (Note, too, that none of the gospels calls it a "hill"; it is just a "place.")

As we have seen before, this passage is a tissue of quotations from Psalms 69 and 22—the details of the gall, the division of garments, and, later, the derision of the bystanders. Sour wine was often given to the condemned as a painkiller, frequently by pious ladies along his way as an attempt at compassion. The soldiers didn't mind, since the less their victim struggled, the sooner the job would be done. Luke mentions it later in v. 36.

Jesus refuses the painkiller, partly to refuse all supports in his lonely and deserted battle, partly perhaps to fulfill his own prophecy at the Last Supper that he would not drink wine again until he drank new wine in the kingdom—which is now only three hours from fulfilment.

In all three cases, even in Mark who rarely shrinks from rude details, the crucifixion itself is stated in the fewest possible words: "They crucified him." There are no details so dear to preachers, like the ringing of the hammer blows and the blood. None of the four—including John—even mentions nails, and Jesus' nakedness is described only indirectly with references to the division of his garments. It is, after all, the painful degradation of their king.

2. Luke is in substantial agreement with the others, paralleling the details of Simon of Cyrene, the place, and the division of garments. He anticipates them by introducing Jesus' fellow criminals and postpones the offering of the sour drink. But Luke has two important and every typical additions.

The first is the women of Jerusalem. In general, Luke's gospel is more sensitive to women, not only showing them as willing to accept discipleship but also, as here, being the only ones with the courage to mourn Jesus publicly. Roman law forbade public mourning at the death of a criminal, especially for one convicted of treason. (Whether the women are Christian converts or Jewish is not clear, but their title "women of Jerusalem" suggests the latter.)

But in Luke's eyes, the tragedy is not for Jesus; he is about to inaugurate his kingdom of reversal. The tragedy is on the side of Israel. As at his arrest in Luke, Jesus is shown seeking not so much to be consoled as to console. "The days are coming" could be a prediction that Jerusalem is headed for literal destruction, which Luke knows it was. But also the prophet Hosea had spoken of Israel's predicament at being without a king and then (10:8) predicted, "the idolatrous high places will be destroyed . . . then they will say to the mountains, 'Cover us!' and to the hills, 'Fall on us!'" It is typical apocalyptic imagery for the end time and the inauguration of the new kingdom. And that is precisely what this moment is.—If these are intended as Christian women rather than, more literally, "daughters of Jerusalem," it is also possible that Jesus was warning the Church that it, too, would suffer the same unjustified presecution as its founder.

"If they do this when the wood is green . . ." Green wood burns with difficulty; dry wood burns quickly. If the innocent Jesus meets the fate that these women see, what will be the fate of those less worthy, those who are truly guilty of the values of the enemy's kingdom? As in much of Luke, this

is an appeal for their conversion, for their recognition of the true values. The Passion is not meant as an occasion for sentiment or for resentment against those responsible for Jesus' sufferings and death. "Weep not for me, weep for yourselves and for your children." It is Jesus who is mourning for them! He is following the path of the kingdom, and his countrymen are going in the opposite direction.

The second addition—again typical for Luke—is that Jesus, in the midst of this torment and desolation and apparent failure, is not thinking of himself but of his tormentors: "Father, forgive them." This is the Jesus who asked the unthinkable of his followers: turning the other cheek. Up till now, his innocence and dignity have been a silent judgment of his tormentors. Here, incredibly according to the world's values, he forgives his torturers at the very moment they are torturing him. We will see even more of this in Luke in the next section.

C. The Vigil

MATTHEW	MARK	LUKE
[37] And over his head they put the charge against him, which read, "This is Jesus the King of the Jews." [38] Then two robbers were crucified with him, one on the right and one on the left. [39] And those who passed by derided him, wagging their heads [40] and saying, "You who would destroy the temple and build it in three days, save yourself! If you are the Son of God, come down from the cross!"	[25] And it was the third hour, when they crucified him. [26] And the inscription of the charge against him read, "The King of the Jews." [27] And with him they crucified two robbers, one on his right and one on his left. [29] And those who passed by derided him, wagging their heads, and saying, "Aha! You who would destroy the temple and build it in three days, [30] save yourself, and come down from the cross!"	[See v. 38—inscription.] [Vv. 32, 33—other criminals.] [V. 37—"If you are King."]
[41] So also the chief priests with the scribes and elders, mocked him, saying, [42] "He saved others, he cannot save himself. He is the King	[31] So also the chief priests mocked him to one another with the scribes, saying, "He saved himself. Let the Christ, the King of Israel,	but the rulers scoffed at him saying, "He saved others; let him save himself, if he is the Christ of God, his Chosen One!"

of Israel; let him come down from the cross and we will believe in him. ⁴³He trusts in God; let God deliver him now, if he desires him; for he said, "I am the Son of God."

[See v. 48.]
[See v. 40.]
[See v. 37.]

⁴⁴And the robbers who were crucified with him also reviled him in the same way.

come down now from the cross, that we may see and believe.

[See v. 36.]
[See v. 30.]
[See v. 26.]

Those who were crucified with him also reviled him.

³⁶The soldiers also mocked him, coming up and offering him vinegar, ³⁷and saying, "If you are the King of the Jews, save yourself!" ³⁸There was also an inscription over him, "This is the King of the Jews."

³⁹One of the criminals who were hanged railed at him, saying, "Are you not the Christ? Save yourself and us!" ⁴⁰But the other rebuked him, saying "Do you not fear God, since you are under the same sentence of condemnation? ⁴¹And we indeed justly; for we are receiving the due reward of our deeds; but this man has done nothing wrong." ⁴²And he said, "Jesus, remember me when you come in your kingly power." ⁴³And he said to him, "Truly, I say to you, today you will be with me in Paradise."

1. Mark has the same simple style, almost all sentences beginning with "And. . . ."
2. Although Matthew adds one more reference to Psalm 22 to the three in Mark, the two accounts are again substantially the same.

Though there were undoubtedly others, Mark and Matthew mention only three taunts, each representative of a group and each focusing more clearly the meaning of the crucifixion.

In the taunts from the passersby—the ordinary Jewish citizens—the charge echoes from the Jewish trial about destroying the temple. This is ironic to the Christian reader, since Jesus—the new temple—is in fact being destroyed at this very minute. (Luke, who omits the charge from the trial, also omits it here.)

The second taunt, from the priests and elders, echoes the charge at the Roman trial about upsurping kingship. It is also laced with ironies. It is a cynical admission that Jesus spent his whole public life doing nothing but helping the helpless, and now he himself is helpless. Then there is the equally scornful dare to come down from the cross as their much desired "sign," and then they will believe. Blindly, they do not see that, according to Yahweh's scriptural will, coming down from the cross would prove he was *not* the Messiah!

The third taunt, from the robbers, is not explained. It merely adds to the pathos of the state Jesus is in, reviled even by his fellow sufferers.

3. Luke mentions the other "criminals" earlier, at the moment Jesus is crucified. His enthronment is a twisted, distorted picture of a king, to be sure, with two advisors on either side. It is an even more distorted picture of the Transfiguration, when Jesus stood in all his glory between Moses and Elijah. Kingship is the theme, and distortion here surely shows the difference between worldly values and the kingdom's values. Companionship with sinners was Jesus' way of offering forgiveness.

In Matthew and Mark, Jesus speaks only once from the cross: "My God, my God, why have you forsaken me?" In Luke he speaks three times and, typically for Luke, they are speeches of mercy and dogged trust in the Father. Perhaps it is difficult for us to realize how very much this is an example of the theme of reversal from the world's values. It struck me most strongly when I visited the ruins of Coventry Cathedral in England. It had been pounded unmercifully by the Germans in World War II, and there was nothing left of it but an empty shell. But from the rough rubble, the townspeople had built an altar and behind it, from the half-burned beams, they had nailed together a bare, blackened cross. On the altar were only two words: "Father, forgive."

Luke repeats the same idea later on the lips of Stephen in Acts (9:35) when he becomes the first of many Christian martyrs, and therefore, like his

Master, a model of forgiveness even of his executioners. As proof that this motto has not yet overcome the opposition's mottoes, one need only read the daily actions of nations, businesses, big league athletics, ghetto crime, and on and on. There is only a small remnant, perhaps even within the organized churches, which can freely say, "Father, forgive." Reversal, indeed.

In Greek, the aorist tense of a verb means that the action is done once and for all and is over with (i.e., "He said"); the imperfect tense, on the other hand, means an action is repeated over and over, like a habit or continuing action ("He was saying"). When Jesus said, "Father, forgive them," the verb is imperfect (*elegen*) which indicates that he was saying it over and over and over. It is a tiny detail, but significant. Far from being anti-Semitic, far even from being ruthless with the Jewish leaders, Luke especially offers forgiveness to them.

In the revilings, Luke does not mention the passersby, and restricts the revilings to the rulers, the soldiers, and one of the criminals. He is again at pains to focus the responsibility not on the common people as a nation but on their leaders. The "people" were watching (v. 35); the "leaders" were scoffing.

Note, too, the parallel with the temptations in the desert: "If you are the King of the Jews. . . . if he is the Christ of God . . . Are you not the Christ?" —all the same temptations for Jesus to doubt who he was which the enemy had used before, in the desert. The enemy, through his followers and those who accept his values, is using them again here. Here, the enemy has control of both the religious and the civil "establishments."

Like a good modern cinematographer, Luke establishes his scene with a wide shot of the rulers spread through the crowd, then tightens to the soldiers at the foot of the crosses, then focuses in on the criminals on either side of Jesus. But, as with the other two synoptics, all of the taunts are variations of the same one: "If you're so big, pull off a miracle—while we watch." I am reminded again of a personal experience at Lourdes, the sickening look of bored expectation on the faces of "pilgrims," watching the sick, hoping for a miracle they could tell about at home. It was not the prayer of people of faith trying to believe though doubtful.

Luke alone, again typically for the gospel of the Prodigal and the Good Samaritan, tells the story of the repentant criminal. Luke's is the gospel of great pardons. As he had done on the way to Golgotha with the women of Jerusalem, Jesus holds out hope even here in this hopeless place. With a reversal which one comes to expect in the gospels, it is from the mouth of a

condemned criminal that the truth comes when he asks to be remembered in Jesus' kingdom.

This moment sums up all of Luke's theology: We share the fate of Jesus, even though he is innocent and we are guilty of the values of the world. The turnabout, the conversion, will bring this treatment from the enemy.

Rarely in the gospels is our Lord called by his name, "Jesus," which means "Yahweh is salvation." Twice in Luke it comes from those possessed by demons and crying out for mercy from the savior. Twice it is used when people cry out for healing. Here, too, it is a cry for mercy, for healing, for a savior— not in the taunting terms of the unrepentant thief but in humble faith.

In so doing, the "good thief" resolves the question which has underlain the trials and the taunts of Luke's Passion account: *"Who are you?"* With an act of faith, the least likely person in the scene declares that Jesus is the savior whose kingdom is more real than the world.

Salvation comes in the very act of seeing and acknowledging that! Once again, Luke uses the techniques of Greek dramatists for whom "the *anagnoresis* [i.e., the recognition] is the fullness of the *peripeteia*" (i.e., the turning point). By this they meant that the climactic turning point of a play like *Oedipus* occurs at precisely the moment when the truth finally erupts and must be acknowledged.

And Jesus responds to the thief's recognition of his personal need for a savior. "Today you will be with me in paradise." It will not be in some future end time, but today, immediately. The kingdom begins at Jesus' death, not at the end of the world or when each of us dies. The kingdom is *now*.

And the kingdom consists of "being with" Jesus, not just in his retinue but "with" him; it is the difference between being "alongside" and being "inside."

It will be a "paradise," a word used in secular Greek literature to denote the private gardens of kings. It is also the word used of the place where Adam was at home with Yahweh. That state has returned—not in the literal sense of trees and snakes and serving girls, but in the symbolic sense of seeing values once again through Yahweh's eyes and not through the literalist eyes of the marketplace. Once again, symbols say more than literal language is able to.

At that moment of humble recognition, the good thief was *in* the kingdom, in the reality which God sees and human beings can see only dimly, "through a glass, darkly."

D. The Death

MATTHEW	MARK	LUKE
[45]Now from the sixth hour there was darkness over all the land until the ninth hour.	[33]And when the sixth hour had come there was darkness over the whole land until the ninth hour.	[44]It was now about the sixth hour, and there was darkness over the whole land until the ninth hour, [45]while the sun's light failed; and the curtain of the temple was torn in two.
[45]And about the ninth hour Jesus cried with a loud voice, "Eli, Eli, lama sabachthani?" that is, "My God, my God, why have you forsaken me?" [47]And some of the by-standers hearing it said, "This man is calling Eli-jah." [48]And one of them at once ran and took a sponge, filled it with vin-egar, and put it on a reed, and gave to him to drink. [49]But the others said, "Wait, let us see whether Elijah will come to save him."	[34]And at the ninth hour Jesus cried with a loud voice, "Eloi, Eloi, lama sabachthani?" which means, "My God, my God, why have you for-saken me?" [35]And some of the by-standers hearing it said, "Behold he is calling Eli-jah." [36]And one ran and, filling a sponge full of vinegar, put it on a reed and gave it to him to drink, saying, "Wait, let us see whether Elijah will come to take him down."	
[50]And Jesus cried again with a loud voice and yielded up his spirit.	And Jesus uttered a loud cry and breathed his last.	[46]Then Jesus, crying with a loud voice, said, "Fa-ther, into your hands I commit my spirit!" And having said this he breathed his last.

1. Mark's only difference from Matthew is merely an apparent one: where Mark says, "Eloi, Eloi," Matthew says, "Eli, Eli." The discrepancy is ex-plained by the fact that Mark was quoting Psalm 22:2 in Aramaic and Matthew was quoting it in classical Hebrew. Recall that this is the same psalm which both of them quoted earlier regarding the division of the virtuous

man's garments and the crowds jeering at him. Here they quote the same psalm again: "My God, my God, why have you deserted me?"

It seemed clear that both Matthew and Mark were quoting the psalm previously and putting those details from the psalm into Jesus' situation—whether they happened historically or not—in order that the details of the narrative would themselves give a commentary on the historic meaning of this historical act.

Did Jesus himself actually quote this psalm? Did Mark and Matthew put it into his mouth as a way of showing what this event truly was? Did the historical Jesus at that moment actually feel abandoned? Scholars I have read seem to prefer either the first or second rather than the third—namely, that either Jesus or the evangelists were making a comment with the psalm which would bring out the true meaning of the situation, rather than an actual declaration of inner abandonment. Surely, from Jesus' own mouth, we do have a stark underlining of the rightness of his taunters' accusations.

As a man of faith reading the Passion with the help of the evangelists and the scholars, I personally suspect that—whatever the words which were actually said—Jesus did actually feel doubt. It is true that in Luke, which is the gospel in which Jesus is so often tempted to doubt, this cry is omitted—even though Luke has it available to him from his copy of Mark. But if Jesus was fully human, I cannot imagine him facing this test as serenely as the academicians would like to say he did. The whole point is tied up with the question of whether Jesus was only progressively aware of his own divinity and therefore faced, as all fully human beings must, the agonizing doubts about whether their self-assessments have been correct. (See *Meeting the Living God*, pp. 187–198).

Finally, Mark is the "gospel of challenge." He says with absolute bluntness: "See this? This is the worst. He has given of himself right to the bottom. Can you still believe?" The signs which Mark describes after Jesus' death are surely an indication that Jesus has not been abandoned. Surely, too, the testimony of the pagan centurion shows where Mark stands. But Mark hides nothing, not even the worst. And he says, "All right. There's the truth. Fish or cut bait."

2. Both Matthew and Mark are very similar otherwise.

The hours which all three speak of are not according to our clocks. Roman time was divided into watches during the night and hours during the day. Therefore, the "hours" do not begin until 6:00 A.M. Thus, the third hour is 9:00 A.M., the sixth hour is noon; the ninth hour is 3:00 P.M. (And the

fabled "eleventh" hour of the parable is not an hour before midnight but an hour before quitting time.)

The darkness all three mention could be historical or not, without making much difference in the true symbolic meaning. It is the embodiment in nature of the near-triumph of Luke's "power of darkness." (Though it seems to be a description of an eclipse, this "cannot" happen at the time of the Passover, which is always set at the time of the full moon.)

Elijah is mentioned by both Matthew and Mark but not by Luke. There was a legend in Judaism that, since Elijah was the only one who had been taken up to heaven while still alive (in a "fiery chariot"), he was expected to return at the end time in order to aid the just in their need. You will recall that Luke has already shown Jesus saying more than once that John the Baptist was that Elijah. Here, however, Matthew follows Mark in associating this cry from the psalm with the apocalyptic events of the end time.

The bystanders mistake what Jesus says—which is understandable, since a man who has endured such torture is not too articulate. One of them, perhaps out of compassion, runs to get Jesus a drink of sour wine. But here Mark and Matthew differ. Mark has the man with the sponge himself saying, "Wait, let's see." Matthew has the others stop him. It is possible that Mark's man with the sponge was trying to keep Jesus alive long enough to see if Elijah would come! Either way, the cruelty goes on to the end, since they will not give him any relief—just in case the "big show" would happen if they let him suffer more.

Moreover, none of them says, "He died." He undoubtedly is dead, but it was not a passive yielding to the inevitable. Jesus is active to the end, and when he breathes his last it is an active rendering up of his spirit to the Father. His life does not slip away from him; he gives it.

In Hebrew, Latin, and Greek, the word for spirit (the "I" which animates the body and mind) is the same as the word for breath. In the cosmic sense of the gospels, at this moment, Jesus gives up his own spirit to his new body—the kingdom which from now on will be his presence and embodiment on earth.

3. Luke's only other difference is Jesus' loud cry, "Father, into your hands I commit my spirit!" It is the peaceful, resigned, fulfilled prayer of Psalm 31:4 and 5:

> *Pull me out of the net they have spread for me,*
> *for you are my refuge;*
> *into your hands I commit my spirit,*
> *you have redeemed me, Yahweh.*

MATTHEW	MARK	LUKE
[51]And behold, the curtain of the temple was torn in two, from top to bottom; and the earth shook, and the rocks were split; [52]and the tombs were opened, and many bodies of the saints who had fallen asleep were raised, [53]and coming out of the tombs after his resurrection they went into the holy city and appeared to many.	[38]And the curtain of the temple was torn in two, from top to bottom.	[See v. 45—curtain.]
[54]When the centurion and those who were with him, keeping watch over Jesus, saw the earthquake and what took place, they were filled with awe, and said, "Truly this was the Son of God!"	[39]And when the centurion who stood facing him, saw that he thus breathed his last, he said, "Truly this was the Son of God!"	[47]Now when the centurion saw what had taken place, he praised God, and said, "Certainly this man was innocent!"
[55]There were also many women there, looking on from afar, who had followed Jesus from Galilee, ministering to him; [56]among them were Mary Magdalene, and Mary the mother of James and Joseph, and the mother of the sons of Zebedee.	[40]There were also women looking on from afar, among whom were Mary Magdalene and Mary the mother of James the younger and of Joses, and Salome, [41]who, when he was in Galilee, followed him, and ministered to him; and also many other women who came up with him to Jerusalem.	[48]And all the multitudes who assembled to see the sight, when they saw what had taken place, returned home beating their breasts. [49]And all his acquaintances and the women who had followed him from Galilee stood at a distance and saw these things.

1. Mark, as we saw when we treated most of this segment previously, uses the declaration of the centurion as the climax of his gospel. In fact, he has reserved the term "Son of God" until this moment. In the context of the kingdom theme of the Passion, it is meaningfully ironic that this Roman

gives Jesus the imperial title *"divi filius,"* and the meaning to the Christian reader is even stronger.

2. Matthew, as we noted before, is the only one of the three who adds apocalyptic details beyond the rending of the temple curtain. This curtain was the one which hung before the holy of holies, the inner sanctum which only the high priest could enter. Whether the real curtain was torn or not is unimportant; the evangelists are saying that God is no longer accessible only to the high priests! Access to God is open to any man or woman, through the death of Jesus Christ. The Mosaic cult has been superceded by a cult that will include even Gentiles. Judaism, not Jesus, has been vanquished at this moment. This is the destruction of the temple—not by an act of war or by an abolition but by a replacement: "Another, not made with human hands" (Mark 14:58).

Only Matthew has the apocalyptic signs of the earthquake and the rising of the dead, as we have seen. Matthew makes the centurion's profession of faith a result of these signs; Mark, more impressively, makes it an act of faith in the person of Jesus rather than in the apocalyptic signs.

The women, whom all three evangelists describe, are used in Mark and Matthew as the "official witnesses" of Jesus' death—as they will be the first official witnesses of the resurrection. It is difficult, therefore, to say that the evangelists are anti-feminist. In the three synoptics—with the exception of Luke's vague phrase "all his acquaintances"—there is no mention of a single one of Jesus' male followers having the courage to be present at Jesus' death.

3. Luke is far more controlled and briefer than the other two. He omits, with typical reluctance regarding apocalyptic, the apparent cries to Elijah, the earthquake, and the risen bodies. He lessens the claim of the centurion to a declaration of innocence—he had broken no Roman law. Given the situation, however, this is not a negligible claim. Notice, too, that only Luke shows that the centurion "praised God" before he made even this assertion—and without the provocation of any apocalyptic signs. The only portents Luke retains are the apparent eclipse and the torn curtain from Mark, and he uses them for the same reasons the others do: to place this event into a cosmic framework and to show that the Old Covenant has been replaced.

Only Luke shows many of the witnesses to the execution returning home "beating their breasts." This fits the theme of repentance and conversion which has surfaced frequently in his Passion account (Peter, the women of Jerusalem, the good thief).

In contrast to these Jews and to the centurion, the followers of Jesus merely stand and watch these reactions, numbed.

4. The three evangelists, then, treat this same event from slightly different points of view. For Mark, the meaning of the Passion is that the temple is through and a new temple has taken its place. For Matthew, this is a cosmic moment in which the forces of the kingdom have, paradoxically, triumphed over the forces of the enemy. For Luke, it is the moment when the kingdom comes to existence in a change of *heart* in the people—which is an event as real and as cataclysmic as an earthquake.

SUMMARY OF DIFFERENT EMPHASES
Mark-Matthew

Neither Mark nor Matthew hesitates to show the Roman guards making a fool of Jesus. Mark, after all, was writing for a Roman audience who could at any moment be called upon to undergo the same treatment. Matthew, writing for Jews, need have no fear of sharing the blame with Gentiles. More than Luke, they take care to select details from the Hebrew Scriptures to show that this ill-treatment of the Messiah should not only not be shocking but should indeed have been expected from the consistent pattern of Yahweh's dealings with his favorites.

Delicacy regarding the actual crucifixion is something one expects from Luke, but when all of the clinical details of the process are passed over in silence by both Mark and Matthew—who were only too aware of how it was done—we must draw some conclusions about their silence. It is a moment too great for words—even for mythic words. Nonetheless, both are only too willing to give every group involved in the shameful scene its fair share of the blame: soldiers, priests, elders, and the whole "people" of Israel.

Luke

Once again, Luke's is the "gospel of mercy." He exonerates the soldiers of the mockery and lays it on Herod and the Jewish elders. He shows Jesus taking pity on the women of Jerusalem, and he laments over the punishment this deed will inevitably visit upon them and on their children—not merely in the destruction of Jerusalem, but the treatment of Jesus by his Jewish countrymen did in fact give excuse for the persecutions and pogroms

which God-fearing and mindless "Christians" will visit upon them and upon their children down to our own days. Even in his own pain, Jesus thinks of this meeting on the road as one more chance to call for a conversion of minds and hearts.

It is only Luke, a moment before the climax of his gospel, who shows Jesus uttering, over and over, the two words which sum up his message: 'Father, forgive."

In the conversation between Jesus and the repentant criminal, the gospel reaches its climax. This unlikely man hanging next to Jesus gives the answer to the question which has followed Jesus through his entire public life since the temptations in the desert: his public "Who are you?" And the answer is, I am Jesus, the savior. I will save you from the kingdom of self-centeredness. In recognizing your need and my ability to answer your need, you are in the kingdom. That recognition is the turning point, the conversion.

Finally, at the very end, the inauguration of the kingdom is not accompanied by the literal fulfillment of the bizarre details of apocalyptic. What those fearsome details in Matthew really mean is what Luke pictures more clearly: repentance over the old values and a total turnabout, a total conversion of the heart and mind.

SUMMARY OF SIMILARITIES

(1) All three evangelists agree about Simon of Cyrene following in Jesus' footsteps, sharing his cross. All agree about Golgotha, the refusal of a painkiller, the crucifixion without details, casting lots for Jesus' garments, the inscription proclaiming with terrible irony that Jesus is king of the Jews, the taunts of the bystanders, the two criminals crucified with him. They agree, too, on the time, the darkness, the curtain, the faith of the centurion, and the women who watch.

(2) The reviling, predicted in the psalms (and therefore a sign of the will of God), all show the same thing: the vicious contrast between Jesus' claims and Jesus' present torment. The contrast is there for those who look at this event with the self-centered, literalist, and materialistic eyes of the enemy's kingdom. And, sadly, the cross was jarring to pious, faithful Jews and to sincere Gentiles as well. But to those who understand the mythic terms in which Yahweh has always described the real reality, this event is a triumph of love over self. What is far more important, it is the moment essential for the resurrection, when our brother entered the fulfillment of his mission: to free us from sin and death and to share with us the aliveness of our Father.

Therefore, putting into the mouths of these people at the cross the very taunts with which Yahweh's enemies had reviled his Just One throughout Israel's history is criticism indeed. But it is absolutely typical of the wrenching reversal of values which the kingdom requires and which we have seen is the core of Jesus' own message. If some of the details are fabricated or brought from somewhere else and inserted, they are surely in no way out of harmony with what Jesus himself actually said in his own words throughout his life.

(3) Throughout the three Passion accounts, Jesus has been hounded with taunts about his kingship. Ironically, this is precisely the moment Jesus becomes king—when he saves his people from the fear of death by dying himself. This is the man Matthew and Luke have shown as a baby receiving homage and gifts from humble Jewish peasants and from rich Gentile wise men. In this agony, Jesus is the embodiment of the paradox at the heart of his message: "Unless a grain of wheat fall into the ground and die, it cannot bear fruit."

But the drama is not yet over. We have seen only the climax. The kingdom has just begun.

10

BURIAL AND EMPTY TOMB

The Gospel is a book of reversals. In the first century, it gave a complete turnabout to the literalist expectations about the Messiah. And from then till now, it calls for a 180° turnabout from the values of the world. But the events of this weekend mean far more than that. Its final chapter is the most shocking reversal of all: Jesus has died, and behold—he lives!

Outline

MATTHEW	MARK	LUKE
1. Joseph asks for body.	1. Joseph asks for body.	1. Joseph asks for body.
2. Shroud; rock tomb.	2. Shroud; rock tomb.	2. Shroud; rock tomb.
3. Pilate surprised Jesus is dead so soon.		
4. Women witness burial.	4. Women witness burial.	4. Women witness burial.
5. Jews ask for a guard.		

6. Morning after sab-
   bath, women to
   anoint Jesus.

7. Earthquake; angel;
   guards like dead
   men.

8. Angel.

9. They run in fear to
   tell the others.

10. Jesus meets them.

11. Guards are bribed.

6. Morning after sab-
   bath, women to
   anoint Jesus.

8. Young man.

9. They run in fear to
   tell the others.

6. Morning after sab-
   bath, women to
   anoint Jesus.

8. Two men.

9. They run in fear to
   tell the others.

10. Apostles doubtful,
    but Peter runs to
    tomb.

The Burial

MATTHEW 27:57–61

[57]When it was evening
there came a rich man
from Arimathea named
Joseph who also was a
disciple of Jesus.
[53]He went to Pilate and
asked for the body of
Jesus. Then Pilate or-
dered it to be given to
him.

[59]And Joseph took the
body, and wrapped it in
a clean linen shroud, [60]
and laid it in his own

MARK 15:42–47

[42]And when evening had
come, since it was the
day of Preparation, that
is, the day before the
sabbath. [43]Joseph of Arimathea, a respected
member of the council,
who was also himself
looking for the kingdom
of God, took courage
and went to Pilate, and
asked for the body of
Jesus. [44]And Pilate wondered if he were already
dead; and summoning
the centurion, he asked
him whether he was al-
ready dead. [45]And when
he learned from the cen-
turion that he was dead,
he granted the body to
Joseph.
[46]And he bought a linen
shroud, and taking him
down, wrapped him in
the linen shroud and laid

LUKE 23:50–56

[50]Now there was a man
named Joseph of the
Jewish town of Arima-
thea. He was a member
of the council, a good
and righteous man,
[51]who had not con-
sented to their purpose
and deed, and he was
looking for the kingdom
of God. [52]This man went
to Pilate and asked for
the body of Jesus.

[53]Then he took it down
and wrapped it in a
linen shroud, and laid
him in a rock-hewn

new tomb, which he had hewn in the rock; and he rolled a great stone to the door of the tomb, and departed. ⁶¹Mary Magdalene and the other Mary were there, sitting opposite the sepulchre.

him in a tomb which had been hewn out of the rock and rolled a stone against the door of the tomb. ⁴⁷Mary Magdalene and Mary the mother of Jesus saw where he was laid. [Cf. 16:1]

tomb, where no one had ever yet been laid. ⁵⁴It was the day of Preparation, and the sabbath was beginning. ⁵⁵The women who had come with him from Galilee followed, and saw the tomb, and how his body was laid; ⁵⁶then they returned, and prepared spices and ointments. On the sabbath they rested according to the commandment.

1. Mark and Matthew have a time for the burial which seems impossible. After sundown on Friday, the Sabbath has begun and no orthodox Jew would dare to work, even in such an honorable cause. Rabbinical law allowed the care of a dead body, but not the digging of a grave—thus the haste in securing the cadaver and walling it into a burial cave. Luke seems to have the more likely time sequence, mentioning evening approaching at the end of the work rather than at the beginning. If Jesus died around midafternoon, there was little enough time to secure Pilate's permission, remove the body, bury it, and return home before the Sabbath began.

All three are quite similar in their treatment of Joseph of Arimathea. There are, however, a few tiny differences. Mark says he was a "respected" member of the council who was "looking for the kingdom of God," rather than expecting the literal fulfillment of the messianic prophecies as many of his colleagues were. Mark also inserts the note that asking for the body of Jesus took courage. In a very subtle way he underlines the fact that none of the men who had followed Jesus so closely for three years had that courage. Once again, the early Church did not portray itself overgrandly. There is no "whitewashing" here. However, to do the apostles credit, the historical reason behind this event could well have been that Joseph was the most highly-placed sympathizer they could find to negotiate with Pilate for Jesus' body.

Although all three use exactly the same words for Joseph's request to Pilate (*estato to sōma tou Iesou*) and although Matthew and Luke both have Pilate turning over the *soma* (body) to Joseph, Mark—with typical blunt-

ness—uses the word *ptoma* (corpse). The Jewish laws expressed in the book of Deuteronomy (21:23) forbade corpses to be exposed overnight.

Only Mark has Pilate expressing surprise that Jesus is already dead, since death by crucifixion often lasted two or three days.

Both Matthew and Mark emphasize the placing of the stone—and Matthew says it was a "great stone." Luke later speaks of a stone having been rolled back. This solidifies the barriers to the resurrection and eliminates claims that vandals had stolen the body.

More explicitly than the other two, Mark stresses the fact that the women are witnesses to the fact of the burial, along with Joseph. Further, though, it underlines the fact that more than one person was certain which tomb Jesus was actually buried in. There were countless tombs just outside the walls of Jerusalem. All three synoptics want to make very clear that there was no doubt in their readers' minds about the women going to the *wrong* tomb on Easter Sunday and finding it empty. It is these same women who are witnesses to Jesus' death, to his burial, and to the empty tomb.

2. Matthew sticks very closely to Mark's version, streamlining somewhat by omitting some details, especially the ones which emphasize the work taking place after sabbath had begun. He does, however, note that Joseph is "rich" and does not mention that he was a member of the Council, the Sanhedrin, which had condemned Jesus. It is probable that, since he alone explicitly says that Joseph was a "disciple of Jesus," he either could not picture the Jewish trial with such a man remaining silent or he did not want to confuse his readers with a long explanation.

3. Luke does make the clarification that Joseph, although a member of the Council, was a good and righteous man and had not voted to condemn Jesus. For the sake of his Gentile readers, Luke also clarifies that Arimathea was "a Jewish town."

Although Luke does not yet name the women, he does say that they returned to their homes to prepare the spices for later embalming and stresses explicitly that they would not break the Sabbath injunction against work. Thus, for his Jewish readers, he is showing that these women are law-abiding and therefore trustworthy witnesses.

The Guard at the Tomb

MATTHEW 27:62–66

[62]Next day, that is after the day of preparation, the chief priests and the Pharisees gathered before Pilate [63]and said, "Sir, we remember how the imposter said, while he was still alive, 'After three days I will rise again.' [64]Therefore order the sepulchre to be made secure until the third day, lest his disciples go and steal him away, and tell the people, 'He has risen from the dead,' and the last fraud will be worse than the first." [65]Pilate said to them, "Take a guard of soldiers; go and make it as secure as you can." [66]So they went and made the sepulchre secure by sealing the stone and setting a guard.

1. Only Matthew mentions this guard. It is odd in several ways. First, the Pharisees are shown recalling Jesus' predictions of the resurrection when his own disciples do not seem to. Second, although Pilate has been seen sneering at the Jews and their superstitions, he nonetheless grants a request he must have thought patently absurd—a man rising from the dead? Third, if there was a guard, historically, why would the other evangelists omit mention of it, since it would add one more obstacle that the resurrection could be shown to overcome? However, if this detail were added out of pious legend, there must have been a reason, and the only feasible one is that the Jews later claimed that the body of Jesus had indeed been removed by his disciples. If the Jews of Matthew's time did actually make that claim, however, it would be a clear indication that they, the "prosecution," had also

checked the tomb and found it empty and therefore needed to trump up another explanation for Jesus' body being missing.

The Empty Tomb

MATTHEW 28:1–10

[1]Now after the sabbath, toward the dawn of the first day of the week, Mary Magdalene and the other Mary went to see the sepulchre.

[2]And behold, there was a great earthquake; for an angel of the Lord descended from heaven and came and rolled back the stone, and sat upon it. [3]His appearance was like lightning, and his raiment white as snow. [4]And for fear of him the guards trembled and became like dead men.
[5]But the angel said to the women, "Do not be afraid, for I know that you seek Jesus who was crucified. [6]He is not here, for he has risen as he said. Come, see the place where he lay. [7]Then go quickly and tell his disciples that he is risen from the dead, and behold, he is going

MARK 16:1–8

[1]And when the sabbath was past, Mary Magdalene and Mary the mother of James, and Salome, bought spices so that they might go and anoint him. [2]And very early on the first day of the week they went to the tomb when the sun had risen.

[3]And they were saying to one another, "Who will roll away the stone for us from the door to the tomb?" [4]And looking up they saw that the stone was rolled back, for it was very large. [5]And entering the tomb, they saw a young man sitting on the right side, dressed in a white robe, and they were amazed. [6]And he said to them, "Do not be amazed; you seek Jesus of Nazareth, who was crucified. He is risen; he is not here. See the place where they laid him. [7]But go tell his disciples and Peter that he is going before you to Galilee; there you will see him, as he told you."

LUKE 24:1–12

[1]But on the first day of the week, at early dawn, they went to the tomb, taking the spices which they had prepared.

[2]And they found the stone rolled away from the tomb, [3]but when they went in they did not find the body. [4]While they were perplexed about this, behold, two men stood by them in dazzling apparel,

[5]and as they were frightened and bowed their faces to the ground, the men said to them, "Why do you seek the living among the dead? [6]Remember how he told you while he was still in Galilee, [7]that the Son of man must be delivered into the hands of sinful men and be crucified,

before you to Galilee; there you will see him. Lo, I have told you." [8]So they departed quickly from the tomb with fear and great joy, and ran to tell his disciples. [9]And behold, Jesus met them and said, "Hail!" And they came up and took hold of his feet and worshipped him. [10]Then Jesus said to them, "Do not be afraid. Go and tell my brethren to go to Galilee and there they will see me." [11]While they were going, behold, some of the guard went into the city and told the chief priests all that had taken place. [12]And when they had assembled with the elders and taken counsel, they gave a sum of money to the soldiers [13]and said, "Tell the people, 'His disciples came by night and stole him away while we were asleep.' [14]And if this comes to the governor's ears, we will satisfy him and keep you out of trouble." [15]So they took the money and did as they were directed; and this story has been spread among the Jews to this day.

[8]And they went out and fled from the tomb, for trembling and astonishment had come upon them, and they said nothing to anyone, for they were afraid.

and on the third day rise." [8]And they remembered his word, [9]and returning from the tomb they told all this to the eleven and to all the rest. [10]Now it was Mary Magdalene and Joanna and Mary the mother of James and the other women with them who told this to the apostles, [11]but these words seemed to them an idle tale, and they did not believe them. [12]But Peter rose and ran to the tomb. Stooping and looking in, he saw the linen cloths by themselves, and he went home wondering at what had happened.

Note that in none of the versions is the Resurrection itself described. How could it be? But it certainly must have been tempting, if they were willing to lie.

1. Unlike the other two synoptics, Mark shows the women on the way to the tomb wondering how they will move the stone. It is odd that, although they had seen it in place and had been forced by the Sabbath to remain away but presumably kept pondering it, that they didn't think of this before they set out to the graveyard. It is at least possible that Mark is quietly underlining the fact that it was only these women—and none of the men—who were willing to come even this close to identification with Jesus and his dangerous teachings. Mark doesn't say how the stone was actually removed; they simply arrive and find it done.

As we have seen before, the young man (*neaniskos*) of this passage may echo back to the young man who deserted Jesus in that puzzling little addition to Mark's version of the arrest. The second book of Maccabees (3:26 and 33) uses a white-robed young man as a symbol of an angel or of the presence of God's message, and white robes are frequently used as symbols for heavenly visitations—as with the Ancient of Days in Daniel and Jesus himself at the Transfiguration.

Just as the symbols of the heavenly presence are different in each version, the speech of the messenger(s) is different—although each says exactly the same thing beneath the differing wording: "He is risen; he is not here." Unlike the other two snyoptics, Mark shows the messenger sending the women not only to the disciples but expressly to Peter. If Papias is correct and Mark was indeed Peter's interpreter, this specific inclusion is understandable. In the light of Peter's denials, it is also quietly critical of him that Peter, the boaster, should not be here with these courageous women.

The statement that the women said "nothing to anyone" obviously does not mean that the women refused to tell the story even to the apostles— since they had just been given what they knew was a mission from God. Rather, it means that they told no one else.

There are some who argue that the original version of Mark's gospel ended right here at verse 8. The vocabulary and style of the rest of Chapter 16 seem to some scholars to be too different from Mark's usual language, and they argue that the rest of Mark's gospel (16:9–20) was added perhaps as late as 100 A.D. This would account for the strong divergences in the remaining sections of Matthew and Luke—not having Mark as a common

source. Moreover, it could be typical of the brusqueness of Mark to end right there, saying equivalently, "See! They went to the tomb and he was *gone*! Now—what do you think?"

However, this would have the whole gospel end with the Greek conjunction *gar* ("For . . . ") which seems highly unlikely. Furthermore, the Council of Trent (1546) resolved the question by declaring that the ending of Mark's gospel as we have it today (16:9–20) is indeed to be accepted with the same validity as the rest of Mark's gospel.

2. Matthew says nothing of anointing, and thus he avoids the problem of the women coming without considering how they would get into the tomb. The women came merely "to see the sepulchre."

The earthquake and the angel are, like Matthew's treatment of the crucifixion, apocalyptic symbols which put this moment into the same symbol-matrix as the book of Daniel. Unlike Luke, Matthew doesn't use the explicit title "Son of Man," but his symbols do that for him.

Although Mark and Luke use less dramatic terms than "angel," the radiant white clothing in both of the other versions leaves no doubt that they were using exactly the same symbolism as Matthew.

The most striking difference in Matthew from the others is the actual appearance of Jesus to the women as they were running to tell the apostles. In Mark's version of the story, Jesus appears first to Mary Magdalene "from whom he had cast seven devils"—with a repetition of Jesus' having risen early Sunday and appearing to Magdalene alone (which is one of the reasons some scholars doubt the "authenticity" of the last eleven verses of Mark). Luke's version shows Jesus appearing first to two disciples on the road to Emmaus. John shows Jesus appearing first to Magdalene who, at first, confuses him with a gardener. But in all the versions Jesus appears to others *before* he appears to his eleven chosen apostles. One might say that the purpose is to show Jesus giving this reward to those who not only kept faith in him but had the courage of their convictions—even though he was still willing to give the less courageous another chance. It is worth noting that in Matthew the words of Jesus are substantially the same as the message of the angel.

Matthew is the only one to describe the priests bribing the guards, since he is the only one who describes their being posted at the tomb. It seems that since these soldiers might have gotten into trouble with Pilate as the result of sleeping on duty, this was a Roman guard rather than a Jewish group. They have come to the most interested parties to get them off the hook—and they have chosen well. Obviously, Matthew inserts this story to

combat the rumors going around in his own time that, although the tomb was indeed empty, it must have been his disciples who spirited the corpse away—"and this story has been spread among the Jews to this day."

3. This section and the rest of the gospel of Luke (24:1–53) all take place on a single day. If we had had only Luke's version, we would have no knowledge of a forty-day period of appearances by Jesus. As the *JBC* says, "This is the first day of a new age—Sunday—which the Church will set apart as its new Sabbath of heavenly rest and joy" (44:175).

The bearer of the news of the resurrection in Mark is a young man; in Matthew it is an angel; in John it is two angels; in Luke it is two men in white. This difference in symbols is only surface; all four are using different symbols to express exactly the same reality. Each is making a symbolic attempt to embody the presence of a message from God—which, of course, is not physical itself. The use of men in dazzling white garments as symbols of this presence is also used by Luke elsewhere in both his gospel and his book of Acts (Lk 11:36, 17:24, and Acts 1:10, 9:3, 10:30, 22:6). There is also an echo of Luke's version of the Transfiguration (9:29) when the divinity of Jesus is expressed by his being clothed in garments "brilliant as lightning," standing with two heavenly witnesses (as here at the tomb).

The message at the tomb in Luke is far simpler than the other two versions: "Why do you seek the living among the dead?" There is the gospel message in a nutshell: Jesus lives.

Matthew and Mark show the heavenly messenger directing the disciples to meet Jesus in Galilee, whereas Luke does not. This is in keeping with the whole geographical thrust which gives shape to his double narrative in his gospel and the Acts. The message began in Galilee and moved inexorably toward fulfillment in Jerusalem (Luke's gospel); then it moved equally inexorably away from Jerusalem to Rome (Luke's Acts of the Apostles). There is no turning back. The whole movement of God's plan is from Galilee to the Jews and then, leaving Judaism behind, to the whole world.

As he will do later in this final chapter, in the Emmaus scene, Luke uses this occasion to insist that the Easter event be seen in light of the prophecies *about* the Messiah and *by* the Messiah. The Son of Man of Daniel = the Suffering Servant of Isaiah = Jesus. It had been repeated over and over in the revelation of God's way of doing things that the Messiah was one who must suffer and die in order to save his people. It had been the way of God with Israel. Jesus had prophesied that it would be the way of God with him. Suffering, dying and being reborn are "the way things are"—which is the same as saying the will of God. And, very simply put, this is also the role

each Christ-ian is called on to live: to suffer the tension between the world's values and the kingdom's values, to die to the world and to be rejuvenated in the kingdom.

SUMMARY OF DIFFERENT EMPHASES

The differences are almost all surface ones. The only large differences occur in Matthew who inserts the two episodes with the guards, apparently to combat rumors circulating in Palestine in his own time that—although the body of Jesus was indeed gone from its burial place—there were this-world explanations. He confronts this attack with evidence that the guards were bribed to spread such rumors by the unprincipled priests.

At first reading, the most startling difference in the versions is the fact that each has a quite different way of announcing the fact that the tomb is empty: a young man, an angel, two men, two angels. However, anyone with a knowledge of symbolic language and the use to which we have seen it consistently put in the Old and New Testaments should find no real difficulty with this. The author of Genesis pictured the heavenly presence to Adam as a friend who strolled in his garden. The author of Exodus pictured this presence as a burning bush. Even a non-believer, if he or she has ever been in love, knows that there are experiences and realities which defy being put into words. Only symbols—no matter how inadequate—will suffice.

Therefore, Mark with his puzzling *neaniskos*, Matthew with his apocalyptic earthquakes and angel, and Luke with his two dazzling witnesses are using different symbols to express exactly the same reality: Yahweh has vindicated Jesus by raising him from the dead. These witnesses are surprisingly different to one unacquainted with the full gospel of each author. But even anyone who has seen only the Passions in parallel as we have in these pages can see that the choice of these particular symbols by each evangelist is obviously typical. Mark has used his *neaniskos* for this same purpose before; Matthew has favored unequivocal apocalyptic thunder and earthquake and angels for this same purpose before; Luke has preferred shining garments and double witnesses for this same purpose before.

SUMMARY OF SIMILARITIES

Beneath these surface differences, the three evangelists declare exactly the same truth: Jesus was raised from the dead. Moreover, even the details of the versions are remarkably the same. A highly placed Jew named Joseph

of Arimathea, who was hospitable to the preaching of Jesus, went to Pilate and secured permission to take Jesus' body down from the cross and bury it. Accompanied by women followers of Jesus, he wrapped it in a linen shroud, placed it in a tomb hewn out of rock, and rolled a stone in front of the doorway. The women noted carefully where the tomb was and then returned to their homes to keep the Sabbath.

At dawn on Sunday, after the Sabbath was over, these women—who included Mary Magdalene and another Mary—came to the tomb and found the stone rolled back from the doorway. They experienced a certainty of the divine presence who assured them that Jesus was indeed risen from the dead and that the tomb was indeed empty. They realized, with certainty, that Jesus had told them all along that exactly this would happen, and they returned in haste to tell the others.

Although each of the synoptics diverges from the others on some details more sharply than we have seen in the Passion, one thing is clear: The Apostolic Church apparently saw no need to harmonize these differences—in effect, to choose from the many versions in order to have one happy, consistent story. And if they—who faced the lions for the Resurrection—were not troubled by these differences, then neither should we. The Resurrection is the most stunning event of the New Testament, and indeed of all time. Had any group of us been witness to the empty tomb, a similar difference of recollection regarding details would have been just as inevitable.

11

APPEARANCES OF THE RISEN LORD

Besides the Resurrection of Jesus, there are three other raisings from the dead pictured in the New Testament: Lazarus, the daughter of Jairus, and the son of the widow of Nain. But the raising of Jesus from the dead is different from any of these. The other persons whom Jesus raised all returned to ordinary existence. They came back to *this* life and, presumably, would die again. But Jesus is pictured by the gospels as conquering death. He was not merely revivified; he was transformed. He was restored to *eternal* life which he can now share with those who believe in him.

But how can we accept that? What evidence do we have to trust it? How do we know that the story of the Resurrection was not (1) a hoax or (2) the result of gullible wishful thinking?

The New Testament makes no attempt whatsoever to describe the actual moment of the Resurrection itself—which is interesting. Had the evangelists been frauds, trying to hoax their audiences outside Palestine into believing in a non-existent resurrection, surely they would have invented some dandy scenes complete with names and "sworn testimony" of non-existent witnesses. Who in Rome or Antioch or Corinth could have checked it? And yet,

on the contrary, Paul—who as Saul had sought to unmask this hoax and persecute the Christian community as heretical to Judaism—did in fact investigate and did in fact end up believing. Surely, if there actually was a tomb in which the corpse of Jesus still lay, the Resurrection—and the claims of Jesus and his followers—would have collapsed. But even those Jews who tried to disprove the claims of Jesus' disciples did not deny that his tomb was empty.

There is, however, another possibility. Even if the apostles had been innocent of fraud, could they have been guilty of being naïve or hallucinating, ready to believe anything after the crushing of their hopes on Good Friday? On the contrary, the evangelists don't spare the early heroes of the Church from exactly the opposite charge: infuriating skepticism. As we have seen in Luke, the apostles thought the women's story was "an idle tale." In John's version, even Magdalene's first reaction to the startling emptiness of the tomb was that the body had been stolen. So unthinkable was resurrection to her that, when she encountered Jesus, she was sure he must be a gardener.

As we will see in the concluding chapters of the synoptics, the presence whom the disciples encountered was a radically transformed Jesus. But the important point is that, however transformed, it was Jesus. Whether the events described after the Resurrection are actually historical in every detail or rather an attempt to embody a non-physical reality in physical terms is not important. The disciples had an experience they died rather than deny. Wolfart Pannenberg writes:

> *Something happened in which the disciples in these appearances were confronted with a reality which also in our language cannot be expressed in any other way than in the symbolic and metaphorical expression of the hope beyond death, the resurrection from the dead. Please understand me correctly; only the name we give to this event is symbolic, metaphorical, but not the reality of the event itself. The latter is so absolutely unique that we have no other name for this than the metaphorical expression of the apocalyptic expectation. In this sense, the resurrection of Jesus is an historical event, an event that really happened at that time.*

A further problem arises regarding the synoptics' treatment of the post-Resurrection events. Having become accustomed to the close parallels of sequence in the synoptic Passion accounts, the reader is surprised by the lack of parallel sequence in the accounts of Jesus' apparitions. There is a vague similarity between Mark and Luke, but Matthew—who had some

form of Mark's gospel as well as Luke did—is surprisingly dissimilar. What is even more surprising is that in Luke's version of the gospel, the appearances of Jesus—and the Ascension—occur all on one day: Easter Sunday. However, we read in Acts, which is by the same author: "He had shown himself alive to them after his passion by many demonstrations for forty days."

As we have seen before, 40 is a symbolic number in scripture. Moses was in the desert 40 years before entering the Promised Land; Jesus was in the desert 40 days preparing himself to enter his public life. Furthermore, 40 days was the norm rabbis used for the length of time a pupil would have to stay with him to memorize the rabbi's teaching. In his second treatment of the events after the Resurrection (in Acts), Luke merely mentions them in one sentence rather than describing them in detail. It is likely that he used the number 40 symbolically and not literally or historically. The apostles were prepared for their mission just as Jesus had been for his, just as the students of any rabbi would be. Forty merely is an indirect way of saying that the apostles' teaching was authentically the teaching of Jesus. It may seem odd to our literalist eyes, but the number 40 expresses a quality rather than a quantity.

However, one is still faced with the problem of aligning the various appearances of Jesus in the three synoptics (without even trying to include John's version).

MATTHEW 28	MARK 16	LUKE 24
9–10 Appearance to the women Easter morning	9–11 Appearance to Magdalene Easter morning	34 Story told by others: "The Lord has appeared to Simon (Peter)"
	12–13 "After this," an appearance to "two of them as they were walking in the country"	13–35 Appearance to two disciples on the road to Emmaus; Easter day
	14–18 "Afterwards," appearance to the Eleven at table	36–49 Appearance to Eleven at a meal; Easter night
16–20 Appearance to the Eleven on a mountain in Galilee (later enough to allow for the journey from Jerusalem)	19–20 "After he had spoken to them," the Ascension (without location or time)	50–53 The Ascension, just outside Jerusalem; Easter night

This difference provokes several problems. First, Mark is typically vague about time. "Afterwards" could mean later the same day (as in Luke) or

later that week or month (as in Matthew), and if Matthew had the same edition of Mark as Luke had, why are they so dissimilar? Second, Luke (and perhaps Mark) compacts all the appearances and the Ascension into one day, while Matthew has to stretch his two appearances at least over several days in order to account for the journey from Jerusalem to Galilee. And third, Matthew places the appearance to the eleven many miles north in Galilee while Luke (and perhaps Mark) explicitly places it in Jerusalem.

First, it is perfectly possible that the last twelve verses of Mark are actually an appendix added by a later writer and patterned on Luke. This need not offer any problem of acceptance since, after all, the gospels themselves are compilations of other writings and of oral tradition which the evangelists in large part merely collected and arranged in their own sequences. Just because the later editor came after Mark rather than before him makes little difference. John, after all, came thirty or forty years after Mark. Finally, whether the last verses of Mark were put in originally or later, they still more or less parallel Luke.

Second: the time lapse before the Ascension. Luke is a stylist. He brings his whole first book to a compact, clean conclusion, all in one day: the new day. Whether the appearances of Jesus historically took place in one day (as in his gospel) or over forty days (as in Acts) is of no importance to him at all. The symbolic "wholeness" of one new day serves him in one place, and the symbolic forty-day training period serves him in the other. Nor are time and location of any pressing interest to Matthew. He wanted to get the eleven to that mountain in Galilee for symbolic reasons, not for historical reasons.

Third: the difference of locations. Again, Luke has a symbolic purpose in bringing his first book to a climax and conclusion in Jerusalem. The holy city is the symbol of Judaism, which will be the first field in which the apostles will continue to sow the seed of the message. In his next book, they will move outward and carry the center of the Christian community from Jerusalem and from Judaism to Rome and the whole world.

Matthew also has a symbolic rather than historical purpose. Perhaps it gave his work a sense of completeness to bring the gospel back to Galilee where it had begun. But the important thing was to get it on a mountain— and perhaps a mountain away from the Jerusalem which symbolized the Judaism Matthew had left behind him. Matthew has a habit of putting important events on mountains, just as the author of Exodus enhanced the meeting of Moses and Yahweh by setting it on a mountain. Where Luke has Jesus giving the beatitudes sermon on a plain, Matthew sets it on a mount. In the temptation, Luke says that Satan "took him up and showed him all the

kingdoms of the world in a moment of time," but Matthew says he "took him to a very high mountain."

In recounting the events after the Resurrection, the evangelists were not writing history in any sense of the term as we are used to it. Unlike Bruce Catton, who must check and recheck dates and times and locations to make his histories of the Civil War as accurate as he can, the evangelists were writing about an *experience* which transcended space and time.

The sequence of events is as clear in St. Paul—the earliest Christian writer and the one closest to the historical events—as any place else:

> *I taught you what I had been taught myself, namely that Christ died for our sins, in accordance to the scriptures; that he was buried; and that he was raised to life on the third day, in accordance with the scriptures; that he appeared first to Cephas (Peter) and secondly to the Twelve. Next he appeared to more than five hundred of the brothers at the same time, most of whom are still alive, though some have died. (I Cor 15:3-7)*

Doubtless Paul omitted the apparitions to the women in order to restrict himself to those whom the Jewish law would accept as responsible witnesses. He concludes his description: "and last of all he appeared to me too; it was as though I was born when no one expected it." The appearance of Jesus to Saul, the disbeliever, was the authentication of the mission and teaching of Paul, the apostle to the Gentiles.

The Conclusion of Mark

[9]Now when he rose early on the first day of the week, he appeared first to Mary Magdalene, from whom he had cast out seven demons. [10] She went and told those who had been with him, as they mourned and wept. [11]But when they heard that he was alive and had been seen by her, they would not believe it.

Verse 9 is obviously a doubling-back to vv. 1–8, the results of the resurrection—the empty tomb and the young man wrapped in white. This is one of the reasons scholars suspect it is an addition.

It is interesting that Mark explicitates the fact that Magdalene had been exorcised by Jesus. And she had not only been possessed but the subject of a seven-fold possession. And it is to such a woman—not to Peter or to the chosen eleven—that Jesus chooses to appear first.

Unlike the women, those who had followed Jesus were mourning and weeping even after Jesus had been dead three days and despite his promise that he would rise again. Finally, in verse 11, Mark repeatedly underlines the apostles' dogged refusal to believe that Jesus really could fulfill his promise.

Appearances to Two Others

> [12]After this he appeared
> in another form to two
> of them as they were
> walking into the coun-
> try. [13]And they went
> back and told the rest,
> but they did not believe
> them.

This episode is obviously very similar to the appearance in Luke to the two men on the road to Emmaus but, like the appearance to Magdalene in John, written in a much duller style with far fewer details. If this were an appendix dependent on either Luke or John, it is surprising that the later editor would not have merely copied the better versions.

The phrase "in another form" probably does not mean that his appearance was different from the person Magdalene saw. Otherwise, how would they have known it was Jesus? Rather, it must mean that it was a Jesus transformed from the ordinary human person they had been used to during his public life. The same situation occurs more subtly in Luke where the two travelers to Emmaus do not recognize Jesus until he sits down and breaks bread with them.

Once again, Mark underlines the disciple's refusal to believe. Perhaps Mark is saying that only those who do have childlike faith are able to see Jesus—anywhere.

Appearance to the Eleven

¹⁴Afterward he appeared
to the eleven themselves
as they sat at table, and
he upbraided them for
their unbelief and hard-
ness of heart, because
they had not believed
those who saw him after
he had risen. ¹⁵And he
said to them, "Go into
all the world and preach
the gospel to the whole
creation. ¹⁶He who be-
lieves and is baptized
will be saved, but he
who does not believe
will be condemned.
¹⁷And these signs will ac-
company those who be-
lieve: in my name they
will cast out demons;
they will speak in new
tongues; ¹⁶they will pick
up serpents, and if they
drink any deadly thing,
it will not hurt them;
they will lay their hands
on the sick and they will
recover.

This triple apparition is, of course, the climax of this section and is obviously intended as a little object lesson on faith. A former possessed woman
has believed; two unnamed and probably relatively unimportant members of
the community have believed. The reason is that they have seen Jesus. Up
to this time the apostles, who have not seen Jesus, still do not believe. Most
of the audience of the gospel were in the same position as the apostles up to
this moment: They have not seen and therefore find it difficult to believe.
The good news is second-hand. They could put themselves in the apostles'
place and be "upbraided . . . for their unbelief and hardness of heart because they had not believed those who saw him after he had risen." And the
Greek word for upbraided is very strong; it is the same word the thieves
used when they were abusing Jesus on the cross.

As in Matthew, the apostles are given a mission to carry the message beyond the confines of Palestine. The new kingdom which begins on Easter is not to be limited to Judaism but is to be shared with "all creation."

Verse 16 is a harsh saying: Baptized believers will be saved and others will be condemned. Many take it even more strongly than Jesus most likely would have intended it. It is not an assurance that anyone who has had a few drops of water poured on him is home free. There are two parts: Baptism and, more importantly, belief. Furthermore, the condemnation of those who refuse to believe is because of their rejection of the kingdom. One should not conjure up pictures of fiery pits in hell into which God rejects the unbelievers. The very act of rejecting the offered kingdom is the punishment; lack of the true fulfillment God offers his sons and daughters.

The miracles of which the true disciple will be capable—exorcism, speaking in tongues, handling serpents and poison without harm, curing the sick—are signs that they share in the power of Jesus. They need not be taken literally, any more than Peter's power to walk on water should be taken literally. They are symbols which say that the Christian who trusts in Jesus will be able to do what a worldling would think is impossible.

Ascension and Mission

> [19]So then the Lord Jesus, after he had spoken to them, was taken up into heaven, and sat down at the right hand of God. [20]So they went forth and preached everywhere, while the Lord worked with them and confirmed the message by the signs that attended it.

From the vagueness of the time words—"after this," "afterward"—one could assume that, like Luke, Mark presents the Ascension on Easter, thus uniting both Jesus' victory over death and his glorification into a single event.

"The Lord Jesus"—As we have seen, the Hellenistic Jews who translated the Hebrew Scriptures into Greek (the *Septuagint*) used the word *kurios* ("Lord") as the translation of "Yahweh." Thus, the author here is attesting to his faith that Jesus and Yahweh are one and the same in power.

Again, one needn't take the words "was taken up" in a spatial, literal sense, any more than one need take "the right hand of God" in a physical, literal sense. Jesus returned to another way of existing, a reality beyond the power of words to describe except in inadequate symbols. The phrase is taken from Psalm 110: "Yahweh's oracle to you, my Lord, 'Sit at my right hand and I will make your enemies a footstool for you.'"

The disciples set out to evangelize the whole world, i.e., to spread the *euangelion*—the Good News—the gospel of Jesus Christ. And it is the exalted Jesus whose Spirit enlivens them and works through them as the new physicalization of Jesus in the world. And the truth of the message will be confirmed by the fact that believers will lead lives more fulfilled than they had thought possible.

The Conclusion of Matthew

[16]Now the eleven disciples went to Galilee, to the mountain to which Jesus had directed them. [17]And when they saw him they worshipped him, but some doubted. [18]And Jesus came and said to them, "All authority in heaven and on earth has been given to me. [19]Go therefore and make disciples of all nations, baptizing them in the name of the Father and of the Son and of the Holy Spirit, [20]teaching them to observe all that I have commanded you. And lo, I am with you always, to the close of the age."

Again, anyone who goes on an archeological expedition to find out which mountain in Galilee this is would be missing the whole point. It is obviously symbolic.

Remember that up to now in Matthew's version there has been only one

vision of Jesus, that of Magdalene, and the message the women have brought back from the angel at the empty tomb. In verse 17 we see the eleven worshipping Jesus—that is, testifying to his divinity after they themselves have seen him. With the same honesty as Mark's version, Matthew admits that some were still doubtful. This typical doubt is made most clear in John when Thomas becomes the symbol of disbelief.

Verse 18 is the declaration which Mark's version has symbolized with sitting at God's right hand and giving Jesus the title "Lord": Jesus has been glorified; he is again the equal of Yahweh.

Verse 19 is the apostolic commission: to teach and to baptize all men and women. Once the believer has accepted the message, the symbol of his acceptance of the kingdom will be baptism which will signify that the Trinity, in its turn, has accepted him. What they will teach is all that Jesus has commanded: a complete reversal of the world's values and standards. As Matthew has done all along, he shows Jesus as the new Moses who opens up a completely new life, free of the slaveries of the world.

Like Mark, but far more briefly, Matthew testifies that it is Jesus whose Spirit animates the work of the new Christian community. It will be the embodiment of Christ until the seed reaches fulfillment at the end.

The Conclusion of Luke

[13]That very day two of them were going to a village named Emmaus, about seven miles from Jerusalem, [14]and talking with each other about all these things that had happened. [15]While they were talking and discussing together, Jesus himself drew near and went with them. [16]But their eyes were kept from recognizing him. [17]And he said to them, "What is this conversation which you are holding with each other as you walk?" And they stood still, looking sad. [16]Then

one of them, named
Cleopas, answered him,
"Are you the only visitor
to Jerusalem who does
not know the things that
have been happening
here in these days?"
¹⁹And he said to them,
"What things?" And
they said to him, "Con-
cerning Jesus of Naza-
reth, who was a prophet
mighty in deed and
word before God and all
the people, ²⁰and how
our chief priests and rulers delivered him up to
be condemned to death
and crucified him. ²¹But
we had hoped that he
was the one to redeem
Israel. Yes, and besides
all this, it is now the
third day since this hap-
pened. ²²Moreover,
some women of our
company amazed us.
They were at the tomb
early in the morning
²³and did not find his
body, and they came
back saying that they
had even seen a vision
of angels, who said that
he was alive. ²⁴Some of
those who were with us
went to the tomb, and
found it just as the
women had said, but
him they did not see."
²⁵And he said to them,
"Oh, foolish men, and
slow of heart to believe
all that the prophets
have spoken! ²⁶Was it

not necessary that the Christ should suffer these things and enter into his glory?" [27]And beginning with Moses and all the prophets, he interpreted to them in all the scriptures the things concerning himself. [28]So they drew near to the village to which they were going. He appeared to be going further, [29]but they constrained him saying, "Stay with us, for it is toward evening and the day is now far spent." So he went in to stay with them. [30]When he was at table with them, he took the bread and blessed and broke it, and gave it to them. [31]And their eyes were opened and they recognized him, and he vanished out of their sight. [32]They said to each other, "Did not our hearts burn within us while he talked to us on the road, while he opened to us the scriptures?" [33]And they rose that same hour and returned to Jerusalem, and they found the Eleven gathered together and those who were with them, [34]who said, "The Lord has risen indeed, and has appeared to Simon!" [35]Then they told what had happened on

>the road, and how he
>was known to them in
>the breaking of the
>bread.

Perhaps a few pre-notes will help before investigating this little story piece by piece. Remember the psychological setting of this episode—which we, who have heard of the Resurrection, might tend to forget. These two men, like the eleven in the next episode, were harrowed with grief. One can get some idea of how profoundly they were affected if one recalls the three harrowing days which followed President's Kennedy's assassination. Here was a young leader, overflowing with vibrant promise, insanely cut down before the peak of his life, and with him the hopes of the whole nation were dashed. In the same way, the first Christian disciples must have gone through the days after Jesus' death in a dulled haze. Jesus was their hope, and now he was gone.

Also it is good to remember that these were not leaders of the Christian community, just as the women who were the first witnesses to the Resurrection were not leaders. The Church is not equated to the apostles or with their successors in the hierarchy. The Church is made up of just such ordinary folk as the women and these two men.

Furthermore, the Emmaus story is not intended to prove anything. Like so much of Luke's gospel, it is intended to show what the ordinary Christian disciple had to go through to find the risen Christ. Here, in one finely wrought little story, Luke sums up the whole thing: ignorance of the meaning within the Scripture, explanation of the Scripture, the recognition of Jesus, and the breaking of the bread. Just as the two men at the empty tomb had told the women (Lk 23:6), Jesus himself tells these travelers that the task of the disciple is to "remember"—the Scriptures, their personal encounter with Jesus, and the celebration of that encounter in the Eucharist. Further, the whole structure of this story is parallel to the structure of the Mass: Jesus' explanation of the Scriptures parallels the liturgy of the word, and his meal with the travelers parallels the liturgy of the Eucharist.

Finally, the pace of the story is interesting. It begins in a long, slow build-up from a leisurely walk in the country to the liturgical climax. Then, after verse 31, the pace speeds up dramatically. The Emmaus episode takes 22 verses, the appearance to the eleven takes 13 verses, and the Ascension itself takes only 4 very short verses. Obviously, this little story is the central focus of Luke's conclusion to his gospel version. On this first day of the new

era, the point of his concentration is on the relationship between Jesus and the ordinary disciple. Let's look at it in detail:

The two men are walking along "talking and discussing" the events of the preceding Friday. As with the days after the Kennedy assassination, the shock of the news left little else to talk about. Note that Luke takes care to say that "Jesus himself" fell in with them. He does not say "the Lord." In this way, he shows the unity between the risen Christ of faith and the Jesus of Nazareth whom they knew. It is the same Jesus but now transformed. Note, too, Luke's continuing penchant for *two* witnesses.

Their eyes were kept from recognizing him. Again, we see that the story is as much about us as about these two earlier Christians. Jesus was no easier for them to see than he is for us to see. As Frederick Danker says in his book, *Jesus and the New Age*, "What the mind does not anticipate, it does not believe, and in the absence of faith, the eye is blind." Each of the evangelists in his own particular way stresses precisely this in his treatment of the apparitions of Jesus after the resurrection. They "weren't ready for that." Despite the fact that Jesus had told them he would rise, their practical intelligences wouldn't allow them to accept what he had said—perhaps wouldn't allow them even really to hear him. It was only later that they really "remembered." Here again we see the utter reversal of expectations which the message calls for. What the world considers impossible is not impossible to Jesus.

There is a touching note in the sentence, "And they stood still, looking sad." It is the same *note* one finds in the episode in John's version where Mary Magdalene discovered the empty tomb and sat there sorrowing. Here again is a perfect example of what stories and figurative language can do which philosophical and theological treatises cannot. The story of these two men is not intended to prove anything—not even that Jesus had risen from the dead. It appeals not to the intellect but to the feelings, so that the reader can *experience* the truth rather than argue to it.

At Jesus' seemingly natural inquiry, Luke recaps the whole Christian *kerygma*—the irreducible core of the message which we have already seen summarized by St. Paul: "That Christ died for our sins, according to the Scriptures, and that he was buried and that he rose on the third day according to the Scriptures, and that he appeared to Cephas and then to the twelve. . . . " (I Cor 15:3–5).

These men have lived the *kerygma* but have not grasped it. Like so many "born Christians," they have heard only with their ears and not with their hearts. In an almost surly way, they say, "Are you the only one who

doesn't know?" And yet, that is unconsciously ironic, since they themselves don't *really* know.

In v. 19 and later in v. 21, Luke shows that these men had identified Jesus with the new Moses, who redeemed his people from the Egyptians. But it seems that they accepted that parallel too literally, hoping that Jesus would have redeemed them only from the Romans, rather than from the values of the world.

While Jesus was "a prophet mighty in deed and word before God and the people," it was the Jewish leaders who condemned him. As Luke has done throughout this Passion, he carefully separates the guilty Jewish leaders from the Jewish people and from the Romans.

As in v. 19, their hope in v. 21 seems to have been the traditional hope of the Jews for a messiah who would be warrior, king, and priest in a literal, worldly way. In 1:74, Luke shows the father of John the Baptist expressing the hope that the Messiah would "grant us, free from fear, to be delivered from the hands of our enemies"; in 2:38, at the Presentation, the prophetess Anna "spoke of the child to all who looked forward to the deliverance of Jerusalem"; and in Acts 1:6, Luke shows the disciples—even as late as the moment before the Ascension—asking, "'Lord, has the time come? Are you going to restore the kingdom to Israel?'" Jesus had an easier task, it seems, exorcizing demons from the possessed than in exorcizing the literalness from his disciples.

Apparently, though, the two travelers to Emmaus had not completely forgotten Jesus' predictions about his resurrection because they note that it is almost evening of the third day after his death; their hopes—and their faith—are waning.

Even the news of the women was not enough to sustain their shaky hopes and faith. The travelers do not say that the women had had a vision of angels but only that the women *said* they had seen them. They seem to be implying: Who can trust women?

In Jn 20:3–10, we see Peter and John running to the tomb to check the women's story out. The two travelers report that those who went to the tomb found it empty, but "him they did not see." Verse 24 is as unconsciously ironic as lines 15–16. The two speakers themselves have Jesus right with them as they are speaking, and they do not see him either! As the Emmaus story unfolds, we see that blindness is indeed the core of it. The empty tomb does not awaken faith in the resurrection, only an understanding of the Scriptures and actually meeting Jesus can awaken faith. And even under-

standing the Scriptures can come about only in a personal meeting with Jesus—since he is the key to them.

Notice that Jesus upbraids them not for their slowness of mind but their slowness of *heart* in understanding *all* that the prophets had spoken. The Scriptures cannot be understood merely with the critical intelligence; they must be read by the person of faith and trust that the God who created a universe from nothing can indeed do what the world says is impossible. Moreover, Jesus says that everything in the Scriptures had to be understood—not just the predictions of the Messiah who would literally free them from their enemies and offer them new prosperity, but also the sufferings that *always* had fallen on the emissaries of Yahweh. If the Jews had always tormented the prophets and ignored their messages, why should these two men be surprised that they crucified *the* Messenger?

Not only was it to be expected that the Messiah would suffer, it was also "necessary." Luke has shown this before: in 9:22, Jesus says, "The son of Man is destined to suffer grievously, to be rejected by the elders and chief priests and scribes and to be put to death, and to be raised up on the third day." In 17:25, Jesus says, "First (the Son of man) must suffer grievously and be rejected by this generation." In 22:37, quoting Isaiah, Jesus says, "He let himself be taken for a criminal."

It is only through suffering, then, that the Messiah could "enter into his glory." In Luke's version, Jesus has said to the Sanhedrin at the Jewish trial, "From now on, the Son of Man will be seated at the right hand of the Power of God." (22:69) And to the Good Thief, Jesus said, "Today you will be with me in paradise" (23:43). All of these symbols—glory, the right hand of the power of God, paradise—like the clouds carrying the Son of Man in Daniel—say the same thing: the equality of Jesus and Yahweh. The Son of Man who had entered his glory was not to come in literal fulfillment of the prophecies, not in apocalyptic splendor. He was in fact a traveler on the road with them.

As we have seen, "Moses and the prophets" summed up all the Hebrew Scriptures. As we can see from the apostles' sermons in Acts, this was the pattern of their instruction, too: going through the Hebrew Scriptures tracing the dealings of Yahweh with men through an intermediary, all of which culminated in the meeting of Yahweh and men in Jesus.

Jesus appeared in vv. 28–29 to be going further, and doubtless he would have if the travelers did not ask him to stay. He will not force himself on anyone. The two men are still blind (and there is a resonance of this

blindness in the approaching darkness), but they are of good will; they want to hear more. The day is far spent, and it is the last day Jesus has to fulfill his promise to rise again. At this moment, this stranger is their only ray of hope. Later, they remember, "How our hearts burned within us while he talked to us on the road."

As they sat down to eat, Jesus "took ... blessed ... broke ... and gave" the bread to them. At the multiplication of the loaves and fishes in Luke (9:16), Jesus "took ... blessed ... broke ... and gave."

Scholars argue whether the action Jesus performed in this story was indeed a celebration of the Eucharist. They point out that there is no wine mentioned. Further, it is only three days after the first Eucharist, so one could hardly say that the Eucharist is a long-standing tradition. Finally, since only the Twelve were present at the Last Supper, it is not likely that these "outsiders" would have heard of it as anything other than a last meal.

However, we are not getting this story directly from Cleopas and his companion. We are hearing it from Luke, writing thirty or more years later. Granting that it was a custom of Palestine Jews to begin meals with a blessing and a breaking of bread, Luke was writing for Theophilus and, presumably, other Gentiles. Thus, "breaking the bread" could have no other meaning for them than the Eucharist. Later, in Acts, Luke speaks of the Christians of Troas who gathered on the first day of the week to "break bread." Therefore, there is strong indication that the "breaking of the bread" spoken of at Emmaus was intended by Luke to show that these two disciples recognized Jesus in the Eucharist.

It is in the very breaking of the bread that their blindness of heart is cured and "their eyes were opened." The explanation of the Scriptures was not enough; it was only a *preparation* for faith. Earlier we saw that Luke uses the techniques of Greek dramatists for whom "the *anagnoresis* (i.e., the recognition) is the fullness of the *peripeteia* (i.e., the turning point)." By this they meant that the turning point of a play occurs at precisely the moment when the truth finally becomes completely clear to the hero. Just as the repentant thief's recognition of Jesus and his kingdom are the turning point of Luke's gospel, so the recognition by these two men is the turning point of this story. The reader is probably weary of reading that the Gospel is a call for reversal, for *metanoia*. But it is just such a turning point that is brought about in each conversion when the person finally recognizes the truth of Jesus and his message.

And as soon as they recognize Jesus, he vanishes. There is no longer need—for those who have recognized Jesus—either for rational explanations

or for physical signs. Just as he had really been with them as they walked along the road, even though they had not recognized him, so he continues to be with them, in the breaking of the bread, even though they do not physically see him. Their hearts burned within them. And this is a fire that must spread, must be shared.

Thus this little polished gem of a story is the *pattern* of every true Christian's faith: false expectations and doubt, understanding of the Scriptures, the unblinding of the heart, the meeting with Jesus, and the apostolic thrust to share the Good News.

Before this, Luke has said only that Peter went to the tomb and found the grave cloths. Here, following St. Paul, Luke says that Jesus had appeared to Peter. Because of the literary form of the *kerygma* we have seen in Paul (I Cor 15), the statement could well have been a liturgical creed which was current in the Mediterranean communities of Christians. But in vv. 33–35 the two travelers repeat their own experiences: the explanation of the Scriptures along the way and the breaking of the bread. As Luke has said before, Jesus warned the disciples not to look for extraordinary apocalyptic manifestations to prove that the kingdom had begun and that Jesus was still with them. "The coming of the kingdom does not come with signs to be observed, nor will they say, 'Lo, here it is!' or 'There!', for behold, the kingdom of God is in the midst of you" (17:20–21). One does not have rational proof of the kingdom or of the presence of Jesus; instead, he recognizes both in "the breaking of the bread."

Appearances of Jesus in Jerusalem

³⁶As they were saying this, Jesus himself stood among them. ³⁷But they were startled and frightened and supposed that they saw a spirit. ³⁸And he said to them, "Why are you troubled, and why do questionings rise in your hearts? ³⁹See my hands and my feet. It is I myself. Handle me and see; for a spirit has not flesh and bones as you see that I have." ⁴¹And

while they still disbe-
lieved for joy and won-
dered, he said to them,
"Have you anything to
eat?" [42]They gave him a
piece of broiled fish,
[43]and he took it and ate
before them.

[44]Then he said to them,
"These are my words
which I spoke to you
while I was still with you,
that everything written
about me in the law of
Moses and the prophets
and the psalms must be
fulfilled." [45]Then he
opened their minds to
understand the scriptures
[46]and said to them,
"Thus it is written, that
the Christ should suffer
and on the third day rise
from the dead, [47]and
that repentance and for-
giveness of sins should
be preached in his name
to all nations, beginning
from Jerusalem. [48]You
are witnesses of these
things. [49]And behold, I
send the promise of my
Father upon you. But
stay in the city, until you
are clothed with power
from on high."

[50]Then he led them out
as far as Bethany, and
lifting up his hands he
blessed them. [51]While he
blessed them, he parted
from them. [52]And they
returned to Jerusalem
with great joy, [53]and

were continually in the
temple blessing God.

Jesus is just "there." There is no mention of how he entered, no apocalyptic grandeur. Had Luke wanted to impress a gullible audience, he could have padded this simple account with all kinds of rumblings. But he did not. The apostles are "startled, frightened, troubled, questioning." This is hardly surprising. After so many years of hearing the Easter story, we might wonder at the heavy insistence on Luke's part regarding the apostles' fears. All one has to do is put himself in their place. This had never happened before! Of course, he had said it would happen, but he had said so many other confusing things, too. One must realize that this was, for them, an apocalyptic moment—all the more frightening for precisely the reason that it was so commonplace, so matter-of-fact, so "everyday." Had there been earthquakes, it would almost have been easier to comprehend than this simple appearance.

Luke hammers home the point of the Emmaus story by repetition here: Seeing is *not* believing. Acceptance of the Resurrection does not depend on mind-boggling signs. It is not based on rational proof. It cannot be satisifed by the testimony of the women or Peter or the two travelers from Emmaus. It cannot arise even from Jesus' own predictions or even from seeing Jesus appear right in front of you. They *still* doubted. In the end, acceptance of the Resurrection depends on the loving surrender of faith.

Perhaps the apostles did in fact "handle" Jesus as v. 39 indicates. Even so, feeling his very flesh (or any other type of "proof") is still not enough. They were so overjoyed that they literally "couldn't believe their eyes."

In vv. 40–43 there are a couple of oddities for which I have found no satisfying explanation. First, although Matthew sets Jesus' appearance to the eleven in Galilee and Luke sets it in Jerusalem, broiled fish is a rare occurrence in Jerusalem, even today, although it is common in Galilee. Secondly, the whole question of the "physical" properties of Jesus' risen body is puzzling. He is able suddenly to appear in a room and yet he is capable of ingesting physical food.

When Jesus says "While I was still with you," he underlines the difference in the manner of his presence among them now as compared to his presence among them before his death. As in the more extended forty-day version of the appearances which Luke gives in Acts, here he authenticates the apostles' training by the Rabbi himself when Jesus interprets his life and message for them in the light of the Hebrew Scriptures.

In the Emmaus episode, Jesus appealed to their hearts as believers in the Jewish Scriptures and especially in the intuitive insight they received in the breaking of the bread. Here he appeals to their minds. As in the other versions, all the previous appearances are to prepare for this appearance—to the eleven. These are the official witnesses, the authoritative witnesses.

In v. 46 for the third time in Luke's Resurrection narrative, Jesus insists on the necessity of suffering and death for the Messenger of the Most High.

Again, in v. 47 Luke stresses the identity of the power of Jesus and Yahweh. Before, one was sent out in the name of Yahweh; now he is sent out in the name of Jesus. And the message to be preached is not that the Messiah has come in literal fulfillment of the apocalyptic prophecies or in literal fulfillment of their nationalistic hopes. They are to tell the world that the fulfillment of the messianic promise is the forgiveness of sins for those who foreswear the values of the world. This is not a worldly revolution, as Luke as stressed so often. It is no threat to Rome's power. It is, indeed, God's mysterious and gracious revelation of himself in Christ Jesus.

They are to begin with their Jewish neighbors, but they are not to be held back there. This is a Message for the whole world. Unlike the other evangelists, Luke hesitates to show Jesus working with Gentiles during his public life. That is to be the task of the Church. Once he has set his face toward Jerusalem, Jesus never turned back. Now he gives his agents the task of setting their faces toward Rome and the whole world.

The "things" to which these eleven are the official witnesses are the message of Jesus and his Resurrection. Those "things" are summed up as well as any man could by Peter in the quotation from Acts which concludes this chapter. Jesus sends the promise of his Father on them—the authentication of Yahweh himself for their mission. He will give them the power to endure anything for the sake of spreading the Good News.

In four abrupt lines (vv. 50–53), Luke "describes" the Ascension and ends his gospel version. With no suggestion of a long interval of time, Jesus goes to Bethany where the events of the Passion began. As the Messiah-Priest, he blesses them and is gone. Again, there are no apocalyptic clouds or thunderclaps. He is just gone into another way of existing. Joyfully, they return to Jerusalem and continued for quite some time to express their joy in the temple, fulfilling the law. Luke's next volume will show their break, not with the Hebrew Scripture, but with the Hebrew law and its ways.

Then Peter addressed them: "The truth I have now come to realize is that God does not have favorites, but that anybody of any nationality who

fears God and does what is right is acceptable to him. It is true, God sent his word to the people of Israel and it was to them that the good news of peace was brought by Jesus Christ—but Jesus Christ is Lord of all men. You must have heard about the recent happenings in Judea, of Jesus of Nazareth and how he began in Galilee, after John had been preaching baptism. God had anointed him with the Holy Spirit and with power, and because God was with him, Jesus went about doing good and curing all who had fallen into the power of the devil. Now, I and those with me can witness to everything he did throughout the countryside of Judea and in Jerusalem itself: and also the fact that they killed him by hanging him on a tree, yet three days afterward God raised him to life and allowed him to be seen, not by the whole people but only by certain witnesses whom God had chosen before-hand. Now, we are those witnesses—we have eaten and drunk with him after his resurrection from the dead—and he has ordered us to proclaim this to his people and to tell them that God has appointed him to judge everyone, alive or dead. It is to him that all the prophets bear this witness: that all who believe in Jesus will have their sins forgiven through his name" (Acts 10:34–43).

There, in six sentences from the model disciple, you have the whole thing.

PART THREE

On Your Own

12

ON YOUR OWN

By this time, the reader who before was used to reading the New Testament literally should have some facility in sorting out the literal from the figurative in the three versions of the gospel by Mark, Matthew, and Luke. He or she should be able to understand that each of them uses purposeful exaggeration, irony, paradox, extended metaphors and parables, symbols, and—very frequently—allusions to characters and events of the Old Testament.

Around the core message of Jesus and the core events of Jesus' life, each of the evangelists has woven his own myth, by which he hoped to make the message and life of Jesus meaningful for his own audience. It was the men and women of the early Christian community who interpreted that message and life, making explicit what Jesus had only implied, drawing out applications of Jesus' value-system and focusing them on their own unique situations—situations which Jesus himself may not have had to deal with directly during his lifetime. In this way, the Gospel became the gospels.

In the following pages, there are selections from the synoptics which the reader can examine closely, without the tiresome intrusions and amplifications of this author. Like the members of the early Church, the reader has two powers working for him or her: the power of his or her own informed intelligence and the power of the Spirit of Jesus who is present within the Christian community now as he was then. Furthermore, the reader should take advantage of the treasurehouse of information stored in a modern

biblical commentary such as *The Jerome Biblical Commentary*. Moving verse by verse through the three synoptics with the thoroughgoing notes provided by such a volume cannot help but enrich one's reading and hearing of the gospel. It can surely enrich one's prayer. Above all, it can enrich one's life.

There are five passages from the synoptics in the following pages. The first three, to begin with, are brief: the episode of the Transfiguration, the controversy story about the Resurrection, and the parable of the sower. Then there is the slightly longer parable of the wicked tenants. Finally, there is the beginning of Jesus' public life. Here the reader will notice that in parts the three evangelists are parallel; in other parts an episode is treated only by Matthew and Luke (Q); still other parts are proper to Luke alone (L).

Read Mark, then Matthew, then Luke. Note the sub-divisions of the episode by drawing a solid line all the way across the page. Then go back to each small segment and note what is common to all three (especially exact verbal identities), then what is common to two, and finally what is unique to each. With the help of a commentary like the *JBC*, try to determine—knowing at least roughly the personal preoccupations, emphases and audiences of each evangelist—why they agree, why they "disagree." In the end, slowly, meditatively, go back and read the three versions again to put each version "back together again," enriched by your newfound insights.

Then, if you are still courageous, pick up an inexpensive volume which gives the full gospels of all three synoptics in parallel. The one I have used, gratefully, throughout this book has been *Gospel Parallels* by Burton H. Throckmorton, Jr. You can probably get a copy in a theological bookstore for about six dollars.

And now, let me leave you and Mark and Matthew and Luke—and their Lord and ours—alone to discover one another.

1. The Transfiguration

MATT. 17:1–8	MARK 9:2–8	LUKE 9:28–36
[1]And after six days Jesus took with him Peter and James and John his brother, and led them up a high mountain apart. [2]And he was transfigured before them, and his	[2]And after six days Jesus took with him Peter and James and John, and led them up a high mountain apart by themselves; and he was transfigured before them.	[28]Now about eight days after these sayings he took with him Peter and John and James, and went up on the mountain to pray. [29]And as he was praying, the appearance of his

face shone like the sun, and his garments became white as light.

³And behold, there appeared to them Moses and Elijah, talking with him.

⁴And Peter said to Jesus, "Lord, it is well that we are here; if you wish, I will make three booths here, one for you and one for Moses and one for Elijah."
⁵He was still speaking, when lo, a bright cloud overshadowed them. and a voice from the cloud said, "This is my beloved Son, with whom I am well pleased; listen to him." ⁶When the disciples heard this, they fell on their faces, and were filled with awe. ⁷But Jesus came and touched them, saying, "Rise, and have no fear." ⁸And when they lifted up their eyes, they saw no one but Jesus only.

³And his garments became glistening, intensely white as no fuller on earth could bleach them.
⁴And there appeared to them Elijah with Moses; and they were talking to Jesus.

⁵And Peter said to Jesus, "Master, it is well that we are here; let us make three booths, one for you and one for Moses and one for Elijah."
⁶For he did not know what to say, for they were exceedingly afraid.

⁷And a cloud overshadowed them, and a voice came out of the cloud, "This is my beloved Son; listen to him."
⁸And suddenly looking around they no longer saw anyone with them but Jesus only.

countenance was altered, and his raiment became dazzling white.
³⁰And behold, two men talked with him, Moses and Elijah, ³¹who appeared in glory and spoke of his departure, which he was to accomplish at Jerusalem.
³²Now Peter and those who were with him were heavy with sleep but kept awake, and they saw his glory and the two men who stood with him. ³³And as the men were parting from him, Peter said to Jesus, "Master, it is well that we are here; let us make three booths, one for you and one for Moses and one for Elijah"—not knowing what he said.
³⁴And as he said this, a cloud came and overshadowed them; and they were afraid as they entered the cloud. ³⁵And a voice came out of the cloud, saying, "This is my Son, my Chosen; listen to him!"
³⁶And when the voice had spoken, Jesus was found alone. And they kept silence and told no one in those days anything of what they had seen.

2. *The Question Concerning the Resurrection*

MATT. 22:23-33

²³The same day Saddu-cees came to him, who say that there is no res-urrection; and they asked him a question, ²⁴saying, "Teacher, Mo-ses said, 'If a man dies, having no children, his brother must marry the widow, and raise up children for his brother.' ²⁵Now there were seven brothers among us; the first married, and died, and having no children left his wife to his brother. ²⁶So too the second and third, down to the seventh. ²⁷After them all the woman died. ²⁸In the resurrection, therefore, to which of the seven will she be wife? For they all had her." ²⁹But Jesus answered them, "You are wrong, be-cause you know neither the scriptures nor the power of God. ³⁰For in the resurrection they neither marry nor are given in marriage, but are like angels in heaven. ³¹And as for the res-urrection of the dead, have you not read what was said to you by God, ³²'I am the God of Abra-ham, and the God of

MARK 12:18-27

¹⁸And Sadducees came to him, who say that there is no resurrection; and they asked him a question, saying, ¹⁹"Teacher, Moses wrote for us that if a man's brother dies and leaves a wife, but leaves no child, the man must take the wife, and raise up children for his brother. ²⁰There were seven brothers; the first took a wife, and when he died left no children; ²¹and the second took her, and died, leaving no children; and the third likewise; ²²and the seven left no chil-dren. Last of all the woman also died. ²³In the resurrection whose wife will she be? For the seven had her as wife." ²⁴Jesus said to them, "Is not this why you are wrong, that you know neither the scriptures nor the power of God? ²⁵For when they rise from the dead, they nei-ther marry nor are given in marriage, but are like angels in heaven. ²⁶And as for the dead being raised, have you not read in the book of

LUKE 20:27-40

²⁷There came to him some Sadducees, those who say that there is no resurrection, ²⁸and they asked him a question, saying, "Teacher, Moses wrote for us that if a man's brother dies, having a wife but no children, the man must take the wife and raise up children for his brother. ²⁹Now there were seven brothers; the first took a wife, and died without children; ³⁰and the sec-ond ³¹and the third took her, and likewise all seven left no children and died. ³²Afterward the woman also died. ³³In the resurrection, therefore, whose wife will the woman be? For the seven had her as wife." ³⁴And Jesus said to them, "The sons of this age marry and are given in marriage; ³⁵but those who are ac-counted worthy to attain to that age and to the resurrection from the dead neither marry nor are given in marriage, ³⁶for they cannot die any more, because they are equal to angels and are sons of God, being sons of the resurrection. ³⁷But

Isaac, and the God of Jacob'? He is not God of the dead, but of the living."

³³And when the crowd heard it, they were astonished at his teaching.

Moses, in the passage about the bush, how God said to him, 'I am the God of Abraham, and the God of Isaac, and the God of Jacob'? ²⁷He is not God of the dead, but of the living; you are quite wrong."

See 11:18b
See 12:32a
See 12:34b

that the dead are raised, even Moses showed, in the passage about the bush, where he calls the Lord the God of Abraham, and the God of Isaac, and the God of Jacob. ³⁸Now he is not God of the dead, but of the living; for all live to him." ³⁹And some of the scribes answered, "Teacher, you have spoken well." ⁴⁰For they no longer dared to ask him any question.

3. The Parable of the Sower

MATT. 13:1–9

¹That same day Jesus went out of the house and sat beside the sea. ²And great crowds gathered about him, so that he got into a boat and sat there; and the whole crowd stood on the beach. ³And he told them many things in parables, saying: "A sower went out to sow, ⁴And as he sowed, some seeds fell along the path, and the birds came and devoured them. ⁵Other seeds fell on rocky ground, where they had not much soil, and immediately they sprang up, since they had no depth of soil, ⁶but when the sun rose they were

MARK 4:1–9

¹Again he began to teach beside the sea. And a very large crowd gathered about him, so that he got into a *boat* and sat in it on the sea; and the whole crowd was beside the sea on the land. ²And he taught them many things in parables, and in his teaching he said to them: ³"Listen! A sower went out to sow. ⁴And as he sowed, some seed fell along the path, and the birds came and devoured it. ⁵Other seed fell on rocky ground, where it had not much soil, and immediately it sprang up, since it had no depth of soil; ⁶and

LUKE 8:4–8

⁴And when a great crowd came together and people from town after town came to him, he said in a parable: ⁵"A sower went out to sow his seed; and as he sowed, some fell along the path, and was trodden under foot, and the birds of the air devoured it. ⁶And some fell on the rock; and as it grew up, it withered away, because it had no moisture. ⁷And some fell among thorns; and the thorns grew with it and choked it. ⁸And some fell into good soil and grew and yielded a hundredfold." As he said this, he called out,

scorched; and since they had not root they withered away.
⁷Other seeds fell upon thorns, and the thorns grew up and choked them.
⁸Other seeds fell on good soil and brought forth grain, some a hundred fold, some sixty, some thirty.
⁹He who has ears, let him hear."

when the sun rose it was scorched, and since it had no root it withered away.
⁷Other seed fell among thorns and the thorns grew up and choked it, and it yielded no grain.
⁸And other seeds fell into good soil and brought forth grain, growing up and yielding thirtyfold and sixtyfold and a hundredfold."
⁹And he said, "He who has ears to hear, let him hear."

"He who has ears to hear, let him hear."

4. *The Parable of the Wicked Tenants*

MATT. 21:33–46	MARK 12:1–12	LUKE 20:9–19

³³"Hear another parable. There was a householder who planted a vineyard, and set a hedge around it, and dug a wine press in it, and built a tower, and let it out to tenants, and went into another country.
³⁴When the season of fruit drew near, he sent his servants to the tenants, to get his fruit;
³⁵and the tenants took his servants and beat one, killed another, and stoned another.
³⁶Again he sent other servants, more than the first; and they did the same to them,
³⁷Afterward he sent his

¹And he began to speak to them in parables, "A man planted a vineyard, and set a hedge around it, and dug a pit for the wine press, and built a tower, and let it out to tenants, and went into another country.
²When the time came, he sent a servant to the tenants, to get from them some of the fruit of the vineyard.
³And they took him and beat him, and sent him away empty-handed.
⁴Again he sent to them another servant, and they wounded him in the head, and treated him shamefully.
⁵And he sent another,

⁹And he began to tell the people this parable: "A *man* planted a vineyard. and let it out to tenants, and went into another country for a long while. ¹⁰When the time came, he sent a servant to the tenants, that they should give him some of the fruit of the vineyard; but the tenants beat him, and sent him away empty-handed.
¹¹And he sent another servant; him also they beat and treated shamefully, and sent him away empty-handed.
¹²And he sent yet a third; this one they wounded and cast out.

son to them, saying, 'They will respect my son.' ³⁸But when the tenants saw the son, they said to themselves, 'This is the heir; come, let us kill him and have his inheritance.' ³⁹And they took him and cast him out of the vineyard, and killed him. ⁴⁰When therefore the owner of the vineyard comes, what will he do to the tenants?" ⁴¹They said to him, "He will put those wretches to a miserable death, and let out the vineyard to other tenants who will give him the fruits in their seasons." ⁴²Jesus said to them, "Have you never read in the scriptures: 'The very stone which the builders rejected has become the head of the corner; this was the Lord's doing, and it is marvelous in our eyes'? ⁴Therefore I tell you, the kingdom of God will be taken away from you and given to a nation producing the fruits of it." ⁴⁵When the chief priests and the Pharisees heard his parables, they perceived that he was speaking about them.

and him they killed; and so with many others, some they beat and some they killed. ⁶He had still one other, a beloved son; finally he sent him to them, saying, 'They will respect my son.' ⁷But those tenants said to one another, 'This is the heir; come, let us kill him, and the inheritance will be ours.' ⁸And they took him and killed him, and cast him out of the vineyard. ⁹What will the owner of the vineyard do? He will come and destroy the tenants, and give the vineyard to others. ¹⁰Have you not read this scripture: 'The very stone which the builders rejected, has become the head of the corner; ¹¹this was the Lord's doing, and it is marvelous in our eyes.' "

¹³Then the owner of the vineyard said, 'What shall I do? I will send my beloved son; it may be they will respect him.' ¹⁴But when the tenants saw him, they said to themselves, 'This is the heir; let us kill him, that the inheritance may be ours.' ¹⁵And they cast him out of the vineyard and killed him. What then will the owner of the vineyard do to them? ¹⁶He will come and destroy those tenants, and give the vineyard to others." When they heard this, they said, "God forbid!" ¹⁷But he looked at them and said, "What then is this that is written: 'The very stone which the builders rejected has become the head of the corner'? ¹⁸Every one who falls on that stone will be broken to pieces; but when it falls on any one it will crush him."

5. *The Baptism of Jesus*

MATT. 3:13–17

¹³Then Jesus came from Galilee to the Jordan to John, to be baptized by him. ¹⁴John would have prevented him, saying, "I need to be baptized by you, and do you come to me?" ¹⁵But Jesus answered him, "Let it be so now; for thus it is fitting for us to fulfil all righteousness." Then he consented. ¹⁶And when Jesus was baptized, he went up immediately from the water, and behold, the heavens were opened and he saw the Spirit of God descending like a dove and alighting on him; ¹⁷and lo, a voice from heaven, saying, "This is my beloved Son, with whom I am well pleased."

MARK 1:9–11

⁹In those days Jesus came from Nazareth of Gailee and was baptized by John in the Jordan. ¹⁰And when he came up out of the water, immediately he saw the heavens opened and the Spirit descending upon him like a dove; ¹¹and a voice came from heaven, "Thou art my beloved Son, with thee I am well pleased"

LUKE 3:21–22

²¹Now when all the people were baptized and when Jesus also had been baptized and was praying, the heaven was opened, ²²and the Holy Spirit descended upon him in bodily form, as a dove, and a voice came from heaven, "Thou art my beloved Son, with thee I am well pleased."